TAI CHI
THE SUPREME ULTIMATE

TAI CHI
THE SUPREME ULTIMATE

Lawrence Galante

SAMUEL WEISER
YORK BEACH, MAINE

First published in 1981 by
Samuel Weiser, Inc.
P.O. Box 612
York Beach, Maine 03910

ISBN 0-87728-497-0
Copyright © 1981 Lawrence Galante

Typesetting by
Friedland Company
New York, N.Y. 10003

Layout by Alden Cole

Printed in the U.S.A. by
Noble Offset Printers, Inc.
New York, N.Y. 10003

Contents

I wish to dedicate this book to the memory of my late mentor, Cheng Man-ch'ing, who was truly a Grand Master of Tai Chi Chuan.

I also wish to dedicate this book to my Spiritual Master— Sathya Sai Baba, who is the embodiment of the Tao.

Preface

In 1976 I published a book entitled *Tai Chi Chuan—Its Form, Function and Application Revealed (Section 1)*. This manual was originally intended for Tai Chi students already versed in the Tai Chi form. Its intention was to teach correct breathing and to explain form application.

The overwhelming response to that manual and the request to adapt it for beginners in Tai Chi caused me to add specific form directions to the existing photographs. But because the book was now overextending its original purpose, I was feeling less satisfied with the overall work. Tai Chi is such a broad system of study. There is so much to say about it that although I received many requests to release "Section 2" of this work, I decided to start over and present one complete volume with an all-inclusive teaching section and with much expanded text, functional for beginners and instructive for advanced students.

As a student of oriental martial arts, I read the available literature over the years and I have always wondered why there is barely any mention of the spiritual content of these arts which had their origins in reclusive spiritual orders. I undertook an extensive research project at Hofstra University on the history, philosophy and spirituality of Tai Chi Chuan and its interrelationship with other systems of study and with health. Much of that material is included in this text, along with a section teaching the Tai Chi form, which is the most comprehensive and complete to date. It contains: photographs of every inhalation and exhalation posture, weight distribution, foot patterns and directive arrows. It also includes application photos of every major posture so that students can grasp the function of these moves and have a mental image to concentrate upon while doing the form. In addition it contains Push Hands and Ta Lu postures. This book, therefore, is a logical extension of my first book and of my research into the philosophy of Tai Chi.

I wish to give my sincere appreciation to those people who have helped me prepare this book:

—First and foremost to my editor, Betsy Selman, who has helped me at every stage of this work with unrelenting encouragement and excellent advice.

—To my photographer and printer Robert Sullivan.

—To John Beaulieu and Leonard Antonucci for their help and contributions with the Tai Chi research projects.

—To my training partner, John Amira, who posed with me in the application photographs and often supplied me with excellent technical advice.
—To David Knee for proofreading my work at Hofstra University.
—To Pam Beaulieu for typesetting the original draft.
—And to Master T.T. Liang who graciously consented to write the foreword to this book.

In addition, I would like to thank:
—All of my previous martial art instructors, especially Master Cheng Man-ch'ing.
—And Satya Sai Baba, for the spiritual insight He has provided.

A WORD OF CAUTION
Although this book can be an invaluable aid to the serious student, no book should be used as a *basis* of study for Tai Chi. Only a qualified teacher can transmit the essence of Tai Chi Chuan and impart to the student a proper foundation and correct instruction.

Lawrence Galante May 1980

Foreword by Master T. T. Liang

T'ai Chi Ch'uan, commonly called T'ai Chi, is an ancient form of Chinese exercise created about seven hundred years ago by Chang San Feng, a Taoist saint of the Sung Dynasty. The fundamental principles of this exercise fall into four categories: health, self-defense, mental accomplishment, and the way to immortality.

In the Classics of T'ai Chi it is said, "When the lowest vertebrae are plumb erect, the spirit of vitality reaches to the top of the head. When the top of the head feels as if it is suspended from above, the whole body will be light and nimble." This is the way to strengthen the spine, and by strengthening the spine one not only automatically strengthens the internal organs, but the brain itself.

The Chi should be stimulated. After the stimulation of the Chi, it becomes so hot that it penetrates into the bone and becomes marrow. The Chi should sink to the Tan Tien (1 1/3 inches below the navel). When your Chi sinks to the Tan Tien the whole body will be relaxed and the blood will circulate freely through the body. When you practice the Tai Chi postures in this manner for a long period of time, you will enjoy perfect health.

When we have attained perfect health, then we can talk about the second fundamental principle, self-defense or the practical use.

As a result of practicing the postures of T'ai Chi for a period of years, you will develop equilibrium, a firm rooting of the feet. From practicing "Pushing Hands" and the "Two Person Set", you will learn to neutralize, yield, and to lose. Loss leads to gain; small loss brings small gain, big loss, big gain.

After you master yielding, next you must know how to counterattack. Once you know how to counterattack, then you must know the lines of your opponent and how to issue intrinsic energy from the spine. The whole body should act as one unit. As the T'ai Chi Classics state: "You have hands everywhere on your body but it has nothing to do with hands." This is also the way to interpret energy. The T'ai Chi Classics again say, "After you have learned how to interpret energy, the more you practice, the better your skill will be. By examining thoroughly and remembering silently you will gradually reach a stage of total reliance on the mind."

I have had more than ten T'ai Chi teachers. From the point of view of his art, I must say that Professor Cheng Man-ch'ing was the best. Professor Cheng learned T'ai Chi for

9

many years from Master Yang Cheng Fu, the third generation of Yang's T'ai Chi family. Once his teacher told him, "There are quite a few people in this world learning and practicing T'ai Chi. They have to discriminate between the pure and the adulterated because, like taking food, the flavor is entirely different. The arms of the pure T'ai Chi master are like iron bars wrapped in cotton, externally flexible, but internally strong and heavy. When grasping the opponent's hands, as in the Pushing Hands practice, although the hands are very light, the opponent cannot get away from them. When he issues or releases his intrinsic energy from his spine it is like a bullet shooting out of the muzzle of a gun. It is as swift as lightning, prompt and clear cut, like breaking a dry biscuit without exerting the slightest external muscular force. As soon as the opponent feels a slight stir of his body, he has already been pushed more than ten feet with no feeling of pain. When the T'ai Chi master only attaches his hands lightly to the opponent's hands, without even scratching or grasping them, it is as firm as glue, impossible to remove and also causes an intolerable aching and numbness in the arms. On the other hand, trying to subdue or seize the T'ai Chi expert is like trying to catch the wind or seize a shadow, ending up with nothing at all; or like attempting to step on a gourd in the water so slippery as to provide no firm hold or footing." This is the meaning of real T'ai Chi Chuan. Master Yang's words are so accurate and precise that I have often tried them out and they have proven absolutely true. I cannot but respect him from the beginning to the end.

By learning and practicing T'ai Chi for a long period of time as a guide for your daily activities you will find the correct way to deal with people and with yourself. Your hot temper will gradually become mild. Hatred, jealously, anger and all depraved thoughts will disappear and your evil temperament will be reformed, abandoning evil to follow the good. Your mind will be upright and pure, and you will enjoy a happy, peaceful and quiet life.

Life begins at seventy. At that age you will realize that fame, wealth, authority and honor are all dust. You will then purify your mind and lessen your desires so you can fully enjoy your life and appreciate nature. Now I am eighty. Within these ten years I have enjoyed good health, found that everything is wonderful, and that the world is beautiful. Now I want to find the way to immortality. Nevertheless, whether I can become immortal or not is another question. A person's life and death are predetermined. Riches and honors are in the hands of heaven. I strongly believe in cause and effect. While we are living, we must be virtuous and try our best to enjoy our life, appreciate nature and finally wait for our allotment so that we will not have spent the best of our days in vain.

Although the author, Mr. Lawrence Galante, has now only reached his middle age, he has read a great many books and researched widely in many different areas. He compares T'ai Chi with Yoga, the I Ching, the Tao Te Ching, Buddhism, Western Psychology, Shaolin, Hsing-I and more. He has scrutinized his subject and scientifically concluded that T'ai Chi Chuan really is beneficial for health. T'ai Chi is good for men, women and children, young and old, sick and healthy alike. Mr. Galante possesses extraordinary ability and high integrity. He is not only a T'ai Chi expert but also a gifted scientist. He has traveled widely, even as far as Asia, in order to study Eastern philosophy. He is now a Buddha "to be", and I am sure that he will become a Buddha "that is".

I am very pleased that he has written such a rare and good book. After reading it, you conclude that it is like a lighthouse for the ships at sea, or like a signpost along the road for cars on land, or the way to immortality for human beings. I recommend it without reservation to anyone living in this world of tension and desires. It shows the way to longevity and to a peaceful and quiet life.

T. T. Liang May 1980

Tai Chi: The Supreme Ultimate

Tai Chi is the popular abbreviation for T'ai Chi Chuan—pronounced tie chee chuwan (tī chē chōowon). It is translated as "The Supreme Ultimate Boxing System". It is a Chinese system for total self-development and improvement. When done correctly, it affects the body, mind and spirit. It is an exercise for the body, a preventative and curative system of Chinese medicine, and a martial art. For the mind it is an exercise in concentration, will power and visualization. T'ai Chi Chuan is also a system of spiritual meditation and a type of Chinese Alchemy.

The name T'ai Chi Chuan is taken from Taoism. The T'ai Chi—"The Supreme Ultimate" or "The Grand Terminus", is a symbol of the eternal Tao. It is composed of a circle containing one yin[1] and one yang[2] harmoniously interconnected. It signifies everything in creation which is manifested and the duality that is contained in all. The word Chuan means "fist" or "fighting system". Thus T'ai Chi Chuan can simply be defined as the supreme ultimate system of boxing or martial art. Chuan also means control. This control implies both self-control and control over a given situation. T'ai Chi Chuan therefore, may be given yet another definition: the supreme ultimate system of self-control in any situation.

The T'ai Chi

13

Origin and History

The Emergence of Shao-lin Temple Boxing

Although Tai Chi Chuan is a Chinese art, its roots can be traced back to India. In 500 B.C., there lived a man in India called Guatama, who was born a prince. He relinquished kingdom, fortune and family to pursue a quest for truth and for the deeper meaning of life. After many years of self-denial, asceticism, meditation, searching and self-inquiry, he achieved what he described as "the highest level possible for one to attain while in his earthly body". From this point on, he was known as "The Buddha"— The Enlightened One. Furthermore, he made a vow that he would not be content with his achievement until he had shared his wisdom with all beings.

> I, having reached the other shore,
> help others to cross the water;
> I, having attained salvation,
> am a savior of others;
> I being comforted, comfort others
> and lead them to the place of refuge.

The Buddha—The Compassionate One, established Buddhist orders throughout India. After his death, the teachings of Gautama, The Light of Asia, spread rapidly eastward. Buddhist Patriarchs left India to teach this doctrine of universal brotherhood, the cessation of suffering, and salvation, to other nations. One famous Patriarch called Padma-sambava crossed the Himalayan mountains, settled in Tibet and founded Tibetan Buddhism. In the sixth century (c.530) a Buddhist monk called Bodhidharma, made a similar journey across the Himalayas and traveled to China to spread Buddha's teachings. He was the son of King Sugandha and was therefore fortunate enough to have the opportunity to study martial arts in India under an old master named Prajhatara. Bodhidharma, also called Ta-mo, established himself in the Shao-lin monastery in Honan Province in northern China and began teaching Buddhist Sutras to

14

his followers. Monks joined the order and the monastery grew. Meditation was a key part of their training and was to unlock many doors in the monks' evolution towards self-mastery. Ta-mo himself was reputed to have sat in meditation facing a wall for nine years. The monks were also instructed in agriculture, herbology and healing. With these skills they helped the sick and hungry. This work helped the monks to better fulfill their vows of saving all beings. Ta-mo discovered that the health of his disciples was deteriorating. They would fall asleep during the sutra studies and they seemed to be unprepared for the rigorous monastery lifestyle. Ta-mo taught that the body and the mind were united; therefore it seemed wrong to him that his monks, who were doing such vigorous mental striving, should be so deficient physically. At this time poor health became a serious threat to their survival because vicious hordes of nomads were sweeping through parts of China, killing and pillaging villages and monasteries. Ta-mo decided to take drastic steps to insure the survival of his Shao-lin order. The monks carried neither weapons nor shields, but Ta-mo declared that through the powers latent within the mind, one could transform the hands into knives, and the arms into shields. Thus to strengthen the body, to defend themselves, and to combat injustice, the monks began to study the way of the righteous fist. Ta-mo's new fighting discipline was a combination of:

1. meditation: the knowledge that the mind is supreme over the body, and that the mind can transform men into invincible fighting machines;
2. the martial arts that he had studied in India;
3. the chinese boxing techniques (which at that time were scattered and disorganized);
4. three sets of exercises taught by Ta-mo for improved health and meditation:

"the eighteen movements of the Ahran Hands", "Sinew Changing", and Marrow Washing Exercises". These exercises were carried over from Indian Avedic medical practices. They emphasized rhythmic breathing and body-stretching maneuvers.

Shao-lin Temple Boxing was born out of this combination. It became a mandatory study in the temple, along with other disciplines to be mastered by the monks. When a monk attained a high level of inner mastery over all the disciplines expected of him in the monastery, including Ta-mo's Temple Boxing; he was called a Kung Fu master. Kung Fu means inner development or mastery, and can be applied to any discipline, for example, meditation; or to any skill, such as playing a musical instrument. Today the popular usage of the term Kung Fu has become virtually synonymous with the Chinese martial arts (Wushu) that the monks practiced. It also may be applied to other martial art forms; Tai Chi Chuan, Hsing-I, Karate, Judo, etc.

As the centuries passed, the boxing system of Shao-lin became formalized into five distinct styles . . . Crane, Snake, Leopard, Tiger and Dragon. These styles were inspired by observing the fighting maneuvers of animals and by imitating their movements. Although conflicting dates are given for this formalization of Shao-lin Boxing, the latest date possible is in the 16th century, by Kwok Yuen, Pak Yook Fong, and Li. Following the creation of the five styles of Shao-lin Boxing, other important styles began to develop. From Crane came Praying Mantis style, from Tiger came Eagle style, from Tiger and Crane, Hung style was invented. Snake and Crane gave rise to Wing Chun, and the list continued to grow.

Crane   Snake   Leopard

Tiger   Dragon

Shao-lin Temple Boxing became famous as the finest system of martial art and was revered all over China. So great was its reputation that martial artists from other countries also wanted to study this system. Shao-lin monks realized that there was great power inherent in these teachings and they were very reluctant to permit the teaching outside of the temple walls.

With the fall of the Ming dynasty (c. 1644 A.D.), outsiders were permitted to enter the temple and learn the boxing art in order to drive out the invading Manchurians.

Wing Chun

Eagle

Praying Mantis

Praying Mantis

Thus Shao-lin boxing left the temple and started to spread throughout China. Later in history, portions of this highly evolved art spread to Okinawa where it was called Shao-lin Ryu, meaning Shao-lin fighting style. When it reached Korea it was called Tai Kuan Do. In Japan it was called Karate, meaning Chinese empty-hand fighting. Even Jujitzu was based upon a style of Chinese boxing called Chin Na which emphasized locks and flips. Chinese Temple Boxing was the mother system which gave birth to the other martial arts in Asia.

Striding Infantryman

(Terracotta, h. 5 feet, 10 inches. Qin dynasty, 221-210 B.C. from: The Great Bronze Age of China: An exhibition from The People's Republic of China. This photograph reprinted with permission from The People's Republic of China and the Metropolitan Museum of Art, New York. Photograph by Seth Joel.)

This statue is historically valuable because it clearly shows that the roots of Chinese Kung Fu Wu Shu go much further back in time than the formalized dates usually attributed to Ta Mo's system of Shao-lin (6th century) or Chang San-feng's system of Tai Chi Chuan (about 1300 A.D.). Note that the statue does not presume to show traditional Kung Fu Wu Shu per se, but only its ancient root heritage with more ancient Chinese Boxing systems. Also note the similarity to the "Shoulder Press" (Form photograph #30) found in the present day Yang style Tai Chi Chuan form.

The Soft School: Tai Chi Chuan

Chang San-feng, a Taoist priest (1279-1368), is generally regarded as the founder of the soft school of boxing. He was supposed to have been a great master of Shao-lin Chuan. It is said that one evening he had a dream in which God taught him how to fight. This dream synchronized with a scene that he witnessed shortly thereafter. A crane and a snake were engaged in mortal combat. He noticed how the snake would recoil to escape the crane's attack and use that same recoil to launch into its own attack. The crane would use its wings to softly cover the snake. He was inspired. He realized the practicality of yielding, pliability and softness. He had felt for a long time that the expenditure of great muscular strength was not in harmony with nature and the theories of meditation. Therefore, he invented his Wu Tang school of meditation and soft martial art. It was named after the Wu Tang mountain range where he taught.

After Chang San-feng, the history of Tai Chi Chuan becomes very vague. It is believed that Chang taught his system to Wang Tsung, who taught Chen Chow Tung, later Chang Sung Chi learned it. But there seems to be many conflicting accounts and dates given by different sources. We can begin to trace the soft school and Tai Chi Chuan much more concretely in the 1600's after Ch'en Wang Ting. The following chart brings the history of Tai Chi Chuan up to date in the U.S.A.[1]

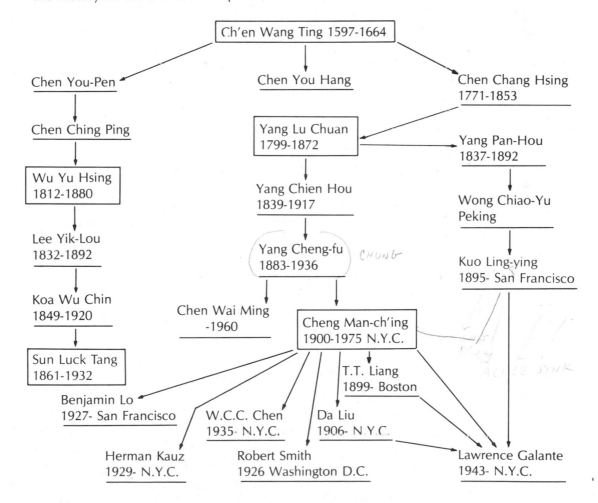

The three main schools of Tai Chi today are Chen, Yang and Wu respectively, started by Chen Wang Ting (1597-1664), Yang Lu Chuan (1799-1872), and Wu Yu Hsing (1812-1880). More recently the Sun style has been gaining popularity; it is named after its founder Sun Luck Tang (1881-1932).

The most popular style of Tai Chi Chuan is the Yang style. My own teacher Cheng Man-ch'ing (1900-1975) learned it from Yang Ch'eng Fu, the grandson of Yang Lu Chuan. Cheng was considered by most to be the greatest exponent of the Yang style in the later half of the 1900's. Cheng was known as the master of the five excellences. He was a master of Chinese medicine and founded the first college of Chinese medicine in Taiwan. He was also a master of calligraphy, poetry and painting. Professor Cheng had tuberculosis as a teenager and was told he would die at an early age. As a desperate measure at age 25, he started to study Tai Chi Chuan. He told us that in six months he stopped spitting blood and in one year his coughing ceased. He continued to practice Tai Chi until his death. It was the beneficial health aspect of Tai Chi that the Professor most wanted to communicate to his followers.

Cheng developed the short Yang form which is much more concise and very popular today. This shortened Yang form is a careful distillation of those moves which contain the most basic principles and which are the most beneficial to one's health. He removed most of the repetitions and some of the more exotic looking fighting movements. The result was a form which took only ten minutes to do instead of the original thirty.

Naturally, these alterations caused the more pedantic practitioners of the Yang style to strongly disapprove. Cheng told his students that his senior brothers, however, approved of his alterations. Cheng's short form opened the door to Tai Chi Chuan to greater masses of people who would not devote the time to learn and to practice such a long series of movements. He trained thousands of people in this short form in both China and the U.S.A. He and his students are most responsible for spreading Tai Chi to the West, and to the United States.

Tai Chi was hardly known outside of China until about fifteen years ago, and then only to connoisseurs of the martial arts. The handful of non-Chinese that had heard of Tai Chi were very vague about the concept of Chi, had no idea of how it could be utilized for self-defense, and had little or no access to qualified instructors. Even in China, martial arts were always veiled in mystery because they were restricted to esoteric circles. Novices were usually accepted from within the family or occasionally from the truly die-hard seekers clammering for initiation and willing to undergo all manner of sacrifice and austerity in order to be admitted into the "inner circle". The Chen family, and later the Yang family practiced Tai Chi Chuan. For many centuries it remained a closed system unavailable to outsiders. The awesome display of martial prowess displayed by Tai Chi Chuan masters during combat or tournaments and the legendary tales of extraordinary abilities, good health and longevity combined to form a kind of magical aura and skill that few could achieve and almost none could understand.

With the Communist revolution in China, came Communist ideals of equality for all. In the eyes of the new government all "elitist practices" had to be discontinued. The esoteric circles of martial art schools were viewed as elitist. The new regime did not have any place for people who would spend the days in full-time practice of martial arts, nor any other arts for that matter, as had been the custom in the old days of China. All people were now required to work in the fields, in the factories and in other communal ventures for the common good of the country. The families with money and property were required to hand over their private possessions to the government for redistribution to the people. The alternative was imprisonment or death. Martial art families adjusted as best they could. Some continued to practice their traditional martial skills in the spare moments available, but since there simply was not the time to teach and train correctly, many of mainland China's most exotic and complex martial skills deteriorated drastically or were lost completely. Others decided to escape from the Communists and flee to Taiwan or Hong Kong, rather than to become proletarians for a regime void of individual artistic expression and talent.

As a result of the emigration from mainland China by Kung Fu masters, such as Cheng Man-ch'ing and others, Chinese martial arts began spreading to other countries in Europe, Asia, and America. Master Cheng particularly wished to teach Tai Chi to non-Chinese students, because he felt that it was an art that should benefit the health of the whole world. He often told his advanced students that he felt that the future of Tai Chi Chuan was in the U.S.A. Although Master Cheng and others did consent to teach their arts outside of China, these arts were not received with overwhelming enthusiasm in their new homelands. People would look upon them with curiosity, fascination and polite interest but only a small handful would actually take the time to study and learn these skills. Was it a martial art or a fancy dance? Was it practical for self-defense? Was it as effective as Karate or Jujitzu? Usually those that did take up the study dropped out before *acquiring* any real adeptness. Even today, the drop-out rate of martial arts students is about 80% within the first three months. People want to learn but are not willing to devote the time and work necessary for practice and improvement in the art.

Ironically, the new Chinese government was destined to reverse its position regarding Kung Fu. It had initially opposed the "old ways" of China, but it did not succeed in changing the people's attitudes about Kung Fu. As the *I Ching* states:

> The town may be changed,
> But the well cannot be changed.[2]

Kung Fu had become like a well with archetypal springs feeding it from deep within the unconscious mind of the Chinese people. They had given birth to Kung Fu over a thousand years earlier and generation after generation had grown to love this unique Chinese boxing exercise. The people just could not say "no more" and turn their backs on Kung Fu overnight. They loved it and still wanted it. The government finally decided to do some research on Kung Fu, to see if there would be any scientific justification for permitting its re-entry into the new Chinese system.

This research so convinced the government of Tai Chi's preventative and curative value that it has been reinstated as a mandatory subject of study for everyone in the public schools. Even workers in factories and on farms take daily exercise breaks to practice Tai Chi Chuan. It was also decided to make Kung Fu Wushu a national sport in the communistic spirit of co-operation. Fighting tournaments were banned but form competitions took their place. A random sample of some of the finest Kung Fu forms from the various styles were collected and standardized and the new sport of Wushu was made official. Working people from all over China are now encouraged to study any of these standard forms. We in the U.S.A. were treated to a demonstration of some of these forms when the Wushu delegation from China visited in 1974. Tai Chi Chuan is one of the styles that was standardized and included in their Kung Fu training. Tai Chi Chuan, however, is still regarded as unique among the Kung Fu styles because the form is suitable for young and old and particularly beneficial to health.

It is interesting to note that in 1956 the Peking All China Physical Training Society created a modified Yang style of Tai Chi form which was adapted by the government of China in its national Physical Fitness Program. It is similar but not the same as the one taught by Cheng. It is more symmetrical. What is done on the right side is also done on the left side. Professor Cheng told us that this symmetry could be detrimental to one's health, because the body is not a symmetrical organism.

In an urban society, where people are beset with nervous tension and anxiety, and have little time or energy to devote to conventional, more strenuous forms of exercise, Tai Chi Chuan is ideal. When Tai Chi Chuan is done daily, it strengthens and rejuvenates the body internally. It is non-strenuous, relaxing, fluid and graceful. The slow rhythmic movements, when centered and balanced, revitalize the entire system, promoting health, strength, relaxation and well-being.

Chinese boxing includes two other important styles in the soft school: Pa-Qua and Hsing-i.

PA-QUA CHANG

Pa-Qua Chang (Pa-eight; Qua-direction; Chang-palm). According to the *I Ching—The Book of Changes,* the universe is divided into eight directions. These eight are called the Pa-Qua and are represented by eight trigrams[3]. These eight trigrams correspond also to eight different palm maneuvers which form the basis of this boxing system. These palm techniques are practiced while walking on the circumference of a large circle.

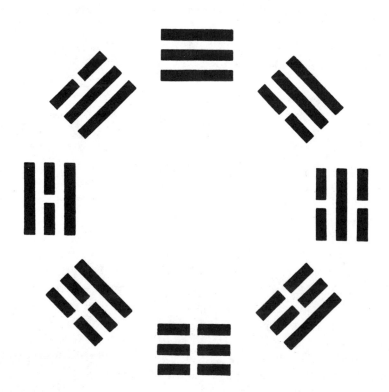

HSING-I

Hsing-i (Mind Boxing) teaches the harmonious merging of thought and action. Taoism teaches that the Tai Chi (Yin and Yang) gives rise to the five basic elements: Fire, Earth, Metal, Water and Wood. Hsing-i is the physical representation of these basic elements. Corresponding to the five elements are the five movements of Pounding, Crossing, Splitting, Drilling and Crushing respectively. The techniques are executed at a high speed and are modeled on the fighting maneuvers of twelve animals—Dragon, Tiger, Monkey, Horse, Turtle, Chicken, Falcon, Swallow, Snake, Dove, Eagle, and Bear—and the five elements.

The Hard and Soft Schools

In Chinese thought, Yin and Yang are present everywhere, and the various martial arts are no exception. Thus we find two major divisions of Chinese pugilism; the Yin or Soft school, and the Yang or Hard school.

The Hard school is most clearly exemplified by Shao-lin Chuan. Relying on strength and speed, the ferocity and martial merit of this style of fighting are very obvious merely from the observation of an expert practicing a "form". A form is a choreographed series of refined and coordinated techniques (blocks and attacks), which simulate actual fighting. Different styles of boxing, that is, Tiger, Mantis, or Crane, etc. may have few or many forms which exhibit techniques peculiar to that given style. Karate and Tai Kuan Do are derivatives of Shao-lin Chuan and are also classified as External-Hard styles of fighting. These styles are very Yang-masculine or aggressive. They usually meet an attacking force with a counter force. Invariably in the Hard styles, the greater force and speed will triumph in a confrontation.

In contrast to this is the Soft-Internal school of boxing. Three main styles of fighting exemplify this system: 1. Tai Chi Chuan, 2. Hsing-i, 3. Pa-Qua. Of these three styles, Tai Chi Chuan is the softest and also the most popular. The main characteristics of the Soft school are that neither speed nor muscular strength is the determining factor of success during practice or in actual combat. When one sees these forms being practiced, it looks like a slow motion dance-like series of movements with no apparent strength being displayed. Yet great force is being generated. This force is not muscular strength, but rather, it is a type of internal force, a psychic energy being released called "Chi". Chi is defined as breath or life energy. (It will be discussed further in a later chapter). The movements of the Soft school are relaxed and pliable. They are Yin, very yielding and feminine. The energy being manifested is not easily discerned by a casual observer. For this reason it is called Internal. It is a more difficult school in which to achieve fighting proficiency. It never meets force with a counter force but rather adheres to and redirects attacking forces. This is termed *neutralizing an attack*. Sensitivity, timing and balance must be mastered, and it usually takes many years of dedicated practice and concentration before self-defense is feasible on a practical level.

The Hard styles of boxing become difficult or impossible to practice on a high level in old age or in poor health. The Soft styles may be successfully practiced at almost any age. By way of example I shall relate a story of one of my own Tai Chi Chuan teachers, Master Kuo Lin Ying. Now in his 90's, he still teaches every morning in San Francisco's Chinatown park at sunrise. As a young boy he started practicing Shao-lin Chuan and achieved great expertise by the time he was a young man. Kuo worked as a body guard and would often travel with goods or money which needed protection. While outside Peking one day, he discovered that a great Tai Chi master called Wong, then 112 years old, lived nearby. Kuo, being anxious to know more about Tai Chi and to prove himself, confronted the famous master and challenged him. Master Wong effortlessly neutralized all of Kuo's attacks, displaying a much higher level of boxing art. Kuo bowed down before his superior and became his student. Master Wong lived to be 123 years old. Master Kuo carries this wonderful tradition and knowledge with him today. He is the living legend of the Chinese martial art community in San Francisco. On my last day of formal training with him, Master Kuo demonstrated his skills to me. He expressed his disdain for Karate, which I had studied for many years, and asked me to attack him. He easily out-maneuvered me and deflected all my attacks. He would either circumvent my blocks and land light punches on my body, or with an effortless touch, send me sailing into a wall. With all my ''hard'' style training, I could neither elude him nor attack him. His soft relaxed system worked. I am very grateful to him for this demonstration, as he very seldom displays this great skill. At this time, Kuo was in his late 80's and I was in my late 20's.

Young and old may practice Tai Chi, as well as athletes or convalescents. It is precisely this characteristic of the Soft schools which accounts for much of its popularity. In fact, Tai Chi Chuan is the most popular form of martial art today because most people are studying it to benefit their health, and not as a self-defense.

Another important consideration is that Tai Chi Chuan is safer to study. When I studied the harder syles, especially Karate, I was injured almost daily, either by hurting myself practicing the jerking kicks and punches, or by being hurt during the sparring. I have never been injured while practicing Tai Chi.

The Tai Chi Classics

During the development of Tai Chi Chuan, a series of treatises were written by Tai Chi Chuan masters about this unique martial art. These treatises are collectively referred to as the *Tai Chi Classics*. They were written by Chan San Feng (13th Century), Wang Chung-Yueh (18th Century). Wu Yu-Seong (19th Century) and Lee I-yu (19th Century). These *Classics* contain the essential principles of Tai Chi Chuan. They give specific instruction to the student on how to maintain his posture, how to execute certain maneuvers, and what to concentrate on while practicing. The *Classics* teach both the mental and physical aspects of this art because in Tai Chi Chuan the mind and body must be aligned so that they become inseparable. Also, although the instructions are often geared towards the martial aspects of Tai Chi Chuan, the points to remember are often multifaceted having meanings which transcend the merely pugilistic aspects of the art.

It is not my intention to reproduce the entire *Classics* here, as this work has been undertaken in several other books now available in English.[1] Rather, what follows is a synopsis of these classic principles.

Basic Principles of Tai Chi Chuan

Relaxation. The entire body must always be relaxed, especially at the chest, shoulders and elbows. Relaxed never means collapsed. The body should be supple, without tension. Exact form must be maintained with a watchful and alert mind.

Emptiness and Fullness. One must clearly distinguish between yin and yang in the body. For example: the left leg is yang when the weight is concentrated there, and the right leg is yin, etc. One must empty the upper portion of the body (above the waist) and render that portion yin, empty and yielding; the legs are yang. When the upper part of the body is empty you cannot be pushed over nor punched; you become like a blade of grass, try to push it over and it will merely yield. You cannot upset its center. This principle applies emotionally and psychologically as well. Aggression or hostility of any kind cannot harm you when you are empty and yielding.

Evenness and Slowness. The form must flow continuously without pause, interruption, acceleration or deceleration. It is often likened to pulling silk from a cocoon; if the continuity is interrupted or if there is any slack or jerk, the silk thread will break. This principle develops continuous force, as opposed to a system like Karate which focusses strength or energy at particular moments. Tai Chi Chuan should be performed as slowly as possible, providing that the other principles are not disturbed. Slowness develops exactness, better balance and patience.

Balance. The spine should be held straight and vertically for optimum strength and balance: no tilting, leaning or twisting. The shifting of weight should flow smoothly like sand through an hourglass. When one leg is full (yang), the other must be empty (yin). If one is double-weighted (weight distributed 50% onto each leg) one's balance can be upset very easily.

Rooting and Sinking. As one learns to relax and sink, one becomes rooted. Sinking means dropping the center of gravity and the center of energy to the lowest possible level. This is done in progressive stages: first lowering the center down from the chest, then dropping it to the waist, next to the legs, and finally down to the soles of the feet. Once someone has reached this point it becomes virtually impossible to upset his balance. In order to sink one must relax the waist and the joints, particularly the knees and ankles. Rooting is the ability to anchor oneself into the ground, like the roots of trees.

Coordination and Centering. The body must move as one complete unit. The extremities reflect and extend the torso movements. There are no isolated sections moving independently. The head follows the body, turning only when the center of the body turns. One must keep his center fixed on the Tan Tien,[2] and all movements must extend from that point. The mind must be coordinated with the body, which is coordinated with the breathing.

Breathing and Chi. Chi means breath-energy or life-energy. From ancient times it was agreed that proper breathing was absolutely essential for the correct performance of Tai Chi Chuan. Tai Chi Chuan incorporates a system of breathing called the "Nei Kung" or "internal merit system." Basically it consists of inhaling whenever the arms are contracted, or pulled backwards, and exhaling whenever they are stretched, raised or pushed forward. Correct inhaling in Tai Chi Chuan means deep abdominal breathing, thus filling the Tan Tien with the vital Chi. Correct exhaling is not merely releasing this air but rather releasing only a portion of it and pressing the rest of this Chi down again into the Tan Tien. When breathing is thus executed the Tan Tien always remain supplied with the life-giving Chi. When such breathing is employed the stomach will naturally expand when one inhales and contract when one exhales. This system of breathing is referred to by Taoists as "Before the Gate of Heaven Breathing".[3]

All breathing is done through the nose, which contains hairs to filter and clean the air before it reaches the lungs. It is also very dangerous to breathe through an open mouth when trying to execute martial art maneuvers, as the teeth and tongue could easily receive serious damage.

Unfortunately, today many Tai Chi students are not taught how to breathe properly when they practice their form. This absence of correct breathing is a severe hindrance to the serious student. My own instructor, Master Cheng Man-ch'ing, would rarely mention breathing, although he was often asked to do so by his students. he would say relax the breathing, keep it natural and rhythmic; but aside from once demonstrating the correct breathing technique for the opening of the form, his stress was elsewhere. In order to arrive at a satisfactory explanation of Master Cheng Man-ch'ing's breathing technique, I was destined to wait until many years after his death, and then the answer, which was a confirmation of the breathing I had learned from my other martial arts masters, came via Master T.T. Liang, the eldest Disciple of Grand Master Cheng Man-ch'ing. Master Liang told me that for years he too had been pestering Professor Cheng for the correct breathing technique. Finally the Grand Master acquiesed and explained that at the moment of a push or strike the air must be exhaled as though shot from a cannon. In this manner all of one's energy is flowing outward towards one's opponent. Master Liang also met the Yang family with whom Professor Cheng studied. He told me that during their pushing practice they would exhale with a loud "Ho" or "Ha". Karate practitioners are famous for screaming at the moment of an attack. This yell, called "Kiya", serves two purposes; it startles the opponent, creating a split second of fear and confusion in which to gain the advantage, and it provides the required exhalation of breath. Similar behavior may be observed in watching a large cat, such as a lion. The great cat will roar as it leaps upon its prey.

To sum up: breathing should be natural and deep, filling up the lowest part of the abdomen. It should always coordinate with the body movements. Inhale when you contract or pull back, and exhale when you expand or strike. Correct breathing will accumulate Chi in the Tan Tien. Once the Tan Tien is full of Chi, it will begin to circulate in the rest of the body, like a pot boiling over. It is this Chi which moves and protects the body.

Concentration. The form should not be performed absentmindedly. Full attention must be given to all of the above principles which apply simultaneously during practice.

In addition to the above principles, the *Tai Chi Classics* contain specific martial art principles, which will be discussed in the chapter "Tai Chi and Self Defense".

Philosophy

The development of Tai Chi Chuan is attributed to Chang San-fang, a Taoist priest. The name Tai Chi is taken from Taoism. Understanding the philosophy of Taoism is an important key in understanding Tai Chi Chuan. "Tai Chi" is a concept of philosophical symbolism; it stands for the primordial emanation of the Tao—The Creation. What is the Tao? A basic tenet of Taoism states emphatically that the Tao cannot be defined.

> The Tao that can be spoken of is not the eternal Tao.
> The name that can be defined is not the unchanging name.[1]

Whatever you name It or call It, cannot really be It. Whenever you think that you have It, you have lost It. Grasp It and It is not to be found. Words can only point in the direction of Tao. To truly understand Tao one has no other recourse but to experience Tao directly. Books, lectures, teachers cannot confer this bliss. The experience of the One is a step that all must take alone. Such an experience will separate the scholar from the mystic, the man with knowledge from the man with wisdom. Faced with this reality from the onset, students of Taoism should at least grasp a direction, or a theme to guide them in trying to comprehend this elusive Tao. The I Ching states:

> This ultimate meaning of Tao is the Spirit, the Divine,
> the Unfathomable which must be revered in silence.[2]

Therefore, in the West we may use words as Way, Spirit, Truth, Ultimate Reality, or God to approximate Tao.[3]

When Tao is translated as Way, it refers to the Cosmic Way of the universe, the order of nature. Originally, Tao means Truth or Ultimate Reality and as such is the equivalent to what we in the West call God. This original, unfathomable Tao was (is) eternally formless and unmanifested, yet complete and perfect. Since It was (is) eternal and infinite, there was no division within Itself and It is called One. From Itself It brought forth the entire cosmos and thus It manifested.

> Tao gives life to beings . . . Tao shapes them . . .
> For Tao is the life and support of all,
> their refuge and shield.
> It makes them arise and grow,
> mature and perfect themselves.[4]

With the creation of the cosmos this Oneness (Tao) became dualistic. This dualism is termed Tai Chi—yin and yang. It is dualistic because It is now individualized and therefore somewhat separate from the original non-differentiated Tao; and also because the instant It became manifest It cast Its own shadow—Its complementary opposite also took form. Yang cast the shadow yin. Or we might say the creation had an unconscious aspect. Thus the entire cosmos is divided into yang and yin, light and darkness, masculine and feminine, positive and negative, day and night, life and death, consciousness and unconsciousness, firmness and yielding. In all things that exist there is yin and yang, form and essence. That which is outer and can be seen, felt, weighed, measured, etc., is the form. What is contained, which cannot be seen, felt, weighed, measured, etc., is essence. Thus in man his material physical body is his form; the invisible life force which sustains and animates the physical body is his essence. Remove the essence, and the form will die and begin to decompose back into elemental form structures, molecules and atoms. It is the essence which makes the form viable and makes it function as a coherent unit of life. Form without essence is dead; essence cannot be manifested without form. Thus when the great invisible Essence, Tao, took form, yin and yang were created; body and soul, matter and spirit were also made.

Original Essence, Tao, has no manifested form. It is called non-existent, the Great Void, Wu Chi. But this Void should be understood to be a very pregnant Void capable of giving birth to all forms in creation. And all of creation, since it arises from It, carries Its Essence somewhere within itself. Without It, the creation could not maintain its existence. The Primal Creation—Tai Chi is essentially Tao. But is is different in that it is Tao with form. Tai Chi, yin and yang, is the basic structure of Tao. Yin and yang are components of Tao.

> Non-existence is called the antecedent of heaven and earth;
> Existence is the mother of all things.
> From eternal non-existence, therefore, we serenely observe
> the mysterious beginning of the Universe;
> From eternal existence we clearly see the apparent distinctions.
> These two are the same in source and become different when manifested.
> This sameness is called profundity. . . . [5]

The Tai Chi

If we examine the diagram of the Tai Chi, we see a circle, which is also a Mandala—an ancient symbol of the self, divided into a light (yang) and a dark (yin) portion. These two are harmoniously balanced and complement each other perfectly. Indeed these aspects are perfectly complementary because the two are actually aspects of the same Original One—Tao. This is symbolized in the circle which surrounds them both and in the fact that each color contains a small circled portion of its opposite within itself. These opposite circles represent the seed of its other half which it is ever ready to give rise to whenever the conditions so merit. It also states that nothing is purely light or dark, good or bad in this relative cosmos; but that all things must be understood to be relative finite blends. This Tai Chi circle should not be looked at as being a static circle but rather one that is constantly spinning. When it is seen in this light, it is easy to see that the yin changes into a the yang and the yang into yin.

> The yang returns cyclically to its beginning;
> the yin attains fullness and gives place to
> the yang.[6]

This idea of eternal interchange between yin and yang forms the basis of the *I Ching—The Book of Changes*. This book and the *Tao Te Ching*, are the two sacred books of Taoism.

The I Ching—The Book of Changes

> That which lets now the dark, now the light
> appear is Tao.[7]

The *I Ching* is considered to be an oracle and one of the oldest spiritual texts in existence. Its origin is unknown. It speaks of the Tao and its interrelationship to life. It teaches that the original unmanifested Tao gave rise to the Tai Chi—creation, yin and yang. The Tai Chi gave rise to the Pa-Qua (eight directions). Each of these directions is represented in the *I Ching* by three lines called a trigram.

These eight trigrams were conceived as images of all that happens in heaven and on earth. At the same time, they were held to be in a state of continual transition, one changing into another, just as transition from one phenomenon to another is continually taking place in the physical world.[8]

These eight trigrams may combine with each other in any combination to form sixty-four hexagrams—six-lined figures. Each hexagram represents a situation or a condition which one may encounter in life.

Each situation demands the action proper to it. In every situation, there is a right and wrong course of action. Obviously, the right course brings good fortune and the wrong course brings misfortune.[9]

When the I Ching foretells future conditions, it is acting as an oracle. When the I Ching advises one what he should do in a given or future situation, that is, what is right action, it becomes a book of wisdom. This book has been studied in China since antiquity and has now become popular in the West. Confucius spent over thirty years studying the I Ching and wrote extensive commentaries on it. It was required study for his students. Lao Tzu must have been familiar with it, since many of the concepts mentioned in the Tao Te Ching are also found in the I Ching.

In the eighteen hundreds, Richard Wilhelm, a Christian missionary from Germany, traveled to China to teach Christianity. He settled with a group of Taoists and began teaching the Gospel (Good News) of Jesus Christ. The Taoists seemed interested and receptive to his teachings and in turn began to teach him the way of the Tao. Thus ensued one of the most important symbiotic exhanges of spiritual information between the cultures of East and West. Wilhelm was so impressed with the wisdom of China that he decided to translate some of the most important spiritual texts into German, the I Ching and The Secret of the Golden Flower.

When he finished translating the I Ching he returned to Europe and submitted his work to Dr. Carl Jung, a physician, psychiatrist and one of the most brilliant minds in the West. Jung was instantly fascinated by the I Ching and set out to understand this work.

I have undertaken it because I myself think that there is more to the ancient Chinese way of thinking than meets the eye.[10]

Interestingly enough, Jung had a strange experience. The wife of one of his patients called him to ask him if her husband was all right. She was worried because a flock of birds had landed on her husband's window. She told him that a flock of birds had landed on her grandfather's window as he lay dying and also on her father's window as he was dying. Birds had become a symbol of death in her family. Jung assured her that her husband was fine, as they had been together earlier that day. Later it was discovered that the husband had indeed died suddenly and that the time of his death coincided with the birds landing on the windowsill. Although it was clear that there was no causal connection between these two events, this incident and others like it caused Jung to postulate the existence of another type of relationship which was acausal or "synchronistic" in his terms. Synchronicity is the coinciding of two or more events in time and space with no apparent causal relationship. He further concluded that it was this exact principle of synchronicity which animated the I Ching and probably other systems of divination, such as astrology, tarot, etc.

> . . . a certain curious principle that I have termed synchronicity, a concept that formulates a point of view diametrically opposed to that of causality. Since the latter is a merely statistical truth and not absolute, it is a sort of working hypothesis of how events evolve one out of another, whereas synchronicity takes the coincidence of events in space and time as meaning something more than mere chance, namely, a peculiar interdependence of objective events among themselves as well as with the subjective (psychic) states of the observer or observers.

> The ancient Chinese mind contemplates the cosmos in a way comparable to that of the modern physicist, who cannot deny that his model of the world is a decidedly psychophysical structure. . . Just as causality describes the sequence of events, so synchronicity to the Chinese mind deals with the coincidence of events.[11]

Another concept at work in the I Ching is what Einstein termed relativity—all things in existence are relative to all other things. The I Ching is strikingly accurate when used for divination—foretelling of the future. When one throws three coins to ask the I Ching a question, the coins will reflect the vibrations of the thrower at that moment (relativity), and the answer given synchronizes with a particular hexagram in the I Ching which will reflect the situation being referred to. The hexagram will analyze the situation, then give advice on how one should proceed for the highest good of the consultant. It was this unique characteristic of the I Ching of giving advice to the consultant which elevated it from merely being a book of divination to a book of wisdom.

> Even to the most biased eye it is obvious that this book represents one long ad-monition to careful scrutiny of one's own character, attitude, and motives.[12]

The I Ching may be used to answer or shed light on any question. It will explain what is going on, whether this condition is harmful or helpful, and it can predict a probable outcome. This outcome, however, is not inflexibly fixed. The future is seen as a natural outcome of the present just as the present is the consequence of the past.

> The reason why we can oppose fate is that reality is always conditioned, and these conditions of time and space limit and determine it. The spirit, however, is not bound by these determinants and can bring them about as its own pur-poses require. The Book of Changes is so widely applicable because it contains only these purely spiritual relationships, which are so abstract that they can find expression within every framework of reality. They contain only the Tao that underlies events. Therefore all chance contingencies can be shaped according to this Tao. The conscious application of these possibilities assures mastery over fate.[13]

Therefore, when the *I Ching* helps a person to understand the present, it is also advising how the future may be altered. Change the trend of the present and the future must change.

The actual procedure of divination is not difficult. The answers that the *I Ching* gives are always correct although one might not always understand them. It may sometimes speak vaguely or it may speak to the querent like a wise counselor, that is, it may disregard the question altogether and give the person much more important advice. For example, one may ask . . . Should I go to Rome on my honeymoon? It may answer . . . Marriage should be avoided, or that a serious flaw in one's personality must be corrected before anything else is to be done. In this way, the *I Ching* speaks as though it has a consciousness all its own.

METHOD

To consult the *I Ching* one may use either 50 yarrow stalks or three coins. The stalk method is complicated and I will not venture to explain it here. The coin method is easier for the average person. One takes three coins, thinks of a question, shakes the coins and throws them down. This is repeated a total of six times. Heads are given a numerical value of 2, tails 3. Each throw is numerically added up and recorded on a piece of paper. The total value of each line is represented as a line, either broken or unbroken, and recorded from bottom to top. Therefore the first line is on the bottom and the last line—the sixth, is on the top. The coins can only add up to one of four numbers: 6,7,8 or 9. 6 and 8 are yin—even numbers, and are represented by a broken line − −. 7 and 9 are yang—odd numbers, and are represented by a straight line ——. Because 7 and 8 are derived from a combination of heads and tails, they are considered stable structures, that is, two heads and one tail are 7; two tails and one head are 8. They are not extremely yin or yang and are, therefore, not in transisiton. They can hold their structure for awhile. 6 and 9 are derived from a combination of either three heads—6, or three tails—9. Since these are extremely yin or yang, they are unstable and about to change over to their opposite. Just as when clouds get too heavy it will start to rain and the clouds will dissipate, so too, if a line becomes too yin, that is, all heads—6—it will change to a yang line. All such lines which are ready to change over are marked with an X or an O in the line in order to distinguish them. The four possiblities are as follows:

6 yin   — X —
7 yang   ———
8 yin   — —
9 yang   —O—

xagram:

tails, one head is 8, yin, stable . . . . —   —
e tails is 9, yang, unstable . . . . —O—
e heads is 6, yin, unstable . . . . —X
tails, one head is 8, yin, stable . . . . —
e tails is 9, yang, unstable . . . .-
tail, two heads is 7, yang, stable . . . .

Since the first throw is written on the bottom and the last on the top the hexagram looks like this:

```
   ————————
   ———O———
   ——   ——
   ——  X ——
   ———O———
   ——   ——
```

The top three lines are called the upper trigram:

```
   ————————
   ———O———
   ——   ——
```

The bottom three lines are called the lower trigram:

```
   ——  X ——
   ———O———
   ——   ——
```

This hexagram represents the answer to the question asked of the *I Ching*. It signifies the present condition. This condition, however, will not remain for very long. It will change. The change will be predictable. This is calculated by reversing all of the extremely yin and yang lines and leaving the stable lines the same. One then goes to the *I Ching* and looks up the appropriate hexagram and reads the solution. Each hexagram is named and numbered and the Wilhelm translation has a handy cross index chart of the trigrams, which makes finding the correct hexagrams easy.

Present		Future
————————		————————
———O———		—— ——
—— ——	changes	—— ——
—— X ——	to	————————
———O———		—— ——
—— ——		—— ——
#59 Dispersion		#52 Keeping Still

Tai Chi Chuan is based upon the principle of the *I Ching*. Just as a hexagram is derived from the one before it so, too, the postures of the Tai Chi Chuan form proceed effortlessly and naturally from the previous postures.

The *I Ching* teaches that the world is always and continuously in movement Chi Chuan form reflects this truth also, in its uninterrupted movements, and without hesitation.

t as the entire cosmos is represented in the *I Ching* as yin and yang the Tai Chi Chuan form should be seen as yin and yang co weight is concentrated on the left foot, it is yang; the empty right foot is yin. When one pushes forward, the front of the body is yang; the back of the body is yin. When the left foot is yang, the left arm is yin and the right arm is yang and vice versa. This knowledge of yin and yang distribution becomes essential for understanding Tai Chi Chuan and its self-defense applications.

The *I Ching* is concerned with the eight primary directions. The Tai Chi Chuan form is designed so that the postures face one of these directions at all times. In addition, all of the major postures of the Tai Chi Chuan form are based on and correspond to, particular hexagrams from the *I Ching*. For example, the opening posture is derived from hexagram "35 Chin—Progress". It symbolizes the sun rising above the earth. The final posture—Cross Hands, corresponds with hexagram "36 Mind I—Darkening of the Light." It symbolizes the sun setting over the earth. Hexagram 35 admonishes the practitioner to develop virtue, and hexagram 36 advises one not to display one's light but to develop humility.

Hexagram 35

The Image

The sun rises over the earth:
The image of progress.
Thus the superior man himself
Brightens his bright virtue.[14]

Hexagram 36

The Image

The light has sunk into the earth:
The image of darkening of the light.
Thus does the superior man live with the great mass:
He veils his light, yet still shines.[15]

These are just two of the many spiritual teachings given by the *I Ching* to promote one's spiritual progress. The Tai Chi Chuan practitioner also must strive to follow such advice in order to practice Tai Chi Chuan on the highest possible level.

The Tao Te Ching by Lao Tzu

Lao Tzu was born in 604 B.C. in the Hunan province in China of peasant parents. He was named Li Erh. During the Chou Dynasty he was keeper of the archives of the library in Lo-Yang. Respected by all for his wisdom, he was given the title "Lao Tzu" which means old sage. Many learned men traveled from afar to speak with Lao Tzu. Confucius, who himself was a great teacher and scholar with many followers, went one day to visit Lao Tzu. Confucius ventured to inquire about the ethical teachings of the old philosophers and to inform the sage of his own viewpoint on such matters. To this Lao Tzu replies:

The philosophers of whom you are speaking, decayed long ago, even if their teachings, as an expression of their times, have been left to us. What is worth knowing, is timeless. If the responsible parties do justice to their time, they are leaders and a blessing for their people; if not, they remain driven ones who stay the progress and perfecting of men.

In vain is every attempt to change men and people by external reform. Tame your vanity, therefore, let go your negligible knowledge! Give up the illusion of the beautiful programs which do not help the people! The people renew themselves out of themselves if they govern themselves in freedom. Man refines himself through his Self: through his indwelling striving for Self-realization. Everything else is vain and useless.

Your way is the way of men; my way is that of heaven. To go my way is to find peace and perfection.

Your way arises from temporality and ends in it. My way leads from the timeless to the eternal; to the fulfillment of the meaning of life.

Your way is the way of action. My way is the way of non-action which does not leave anything undone: the way of stillness and tranquility out of which the right consciousness arises.[16]

It is reported that Confucius was literally dumbstruck after speaking with Lao Tzu, and did not utter a word for three days. Afterwards Confucius said, concerning his talk with Lao Tzu:

> Birds fly, fish swim, animals run, each in its own way. But there are dragons of which no one knows how they rise to heaven. When I spoke with Lao Tzu, I recognized in him a dragon that rises to the highest heavens of wisdom.[17]

The story of this encounter between Lao Tzu and Confucius can provide the student of Taoism with a valuable lesson. Confucius was grounded in the ways of man and the world. Lao Tzu was grounded in the Tao, a lofty spiritual level. Plato called such men Philosopher Kings. Those who made the teachings and ideals of philosophy their very nature and lived in perfect harmony with that knowledge, which comes to them via the higher inner self—the superconsciousness.

Such men have appeared to humanity in every culture and every religion. Their lives serve to inspire and to uplift mankind. They are called wise men, sages, saints, and holy men. They are all united in One Eternal Truth. The language and the symbols may differ to describe this Truth, but that should not surprise us as we have already stated that the Tao is indescribable. Some call it Tao, some the Great Light, some say God, others call it the Great Void.

Lao Tzu was a mystic. Mysticism is the immediate knowledge and experience of Ultimate Reality or God. The specific characteristic attributes of the mystical experience are self-transcendence, union or identification with the Supreme Power of the universe, and the consequent feeling of exaltation or ecstasy. Other important accompanying signs are transcendence of time and space, and a positive change in behavior.

Lao Tzu was in every sense of the word a mystic. Any attempt to translate his work and delete it of mysticism, as is sometimes done, is like removing the cream before serving the milk; that is, removing the spiritual essence which lies beneath the external form of his teachings. It is reputed that at the age of one hundred and sixty, Lao Tzu decided to renounce society and retire to the mountains. Upon reaching the Han-Ku pass, Yin-Hsi, the gate keeper and also a student of his, asked him to leave a record of his teachings for humanity. Lao Tzu left a manuscript of some five thousand Chinese characters (5,280) called the *Tao Te Ching*.

Tao—Way, Truth, etc.
Te—Power, Virtue
Ching—Book, classic

Therefore, the *Tao Te Ching* may be translated as *the classical book of the Way or Truth and its power or virtue.*

Tao is both a noun and a verb meaning that it is both Being and becoming. As a noun it signifies Truth or Ultimate Reality. As a verb it signifies nature and its way of movement, that is to say, the natural laws that are always in operation.

The *Tao Te Ching* is one of the great spiritual writings left as a guide post and a legacy for mankind. It is so simple and simultaneously so complex that it baffles the most brilliant minds. Only the mystic can comprehend its profundity. It is rooted in spiritual eternity and therefore remains timeless and pertinent to any time in man's history or personal development.

Just as the Sermon on the Mount is the essense of Christ's teaching, the Noble Eight-Fold path the core of the Buddha's message, and the *Bhagavad Gita* the essential core of Krishna's message so, too, the *Tao Te Ching* contains Lao Tzu's essential message.

With the exception of the *Bible*, the *Tao Te Ching* is the most translated book in the world.

The *Tao Te Ching* takes most of its illustrations from nature. Lao Tzu taught that nature was man's finest teacher and that man would reach a state of serenity and happiness by living in accordance with the Way of nature. When man contradicts this Way, the inevitable consequence is pain and suffering. The Way for man is to be in accord with nature and with his own true self. Man must harmonize his true nature with the nature of the cosmos. Thus the microcosm (man) and the macrocosm (the universe) blend and become the yin and the yang, balancing and revitalizing one another.

Lao Tzu teaches a contemplative way, where talk is superfluous and example teaches best. It is a way of emptying the self of egotism and the illusion that man governs his world. Man must learn the way of Wu Wei (non action) in which he relaxes completely, thus becoming the living channel for the mysterious supernatural force—Tao. Wu Wei is not laziness, but rather refraining from doing anything which is contrary to the way of the Tao. The Tao is constantly at work benefitting all of its creation; it merely becomes man's duty to trust in Its benevolent power and not interfere with Its Way. Man must practice stillness and meditation. He must learn to relax and then the correct thing will happen as is its nature to happen. A seed changes into a mighty tree because the Tao acts through it. In the same way man can be transformed into a majestic expression of the Tao.

When a man is to take the world over and shape it
I see that he must be obliged to do it.
For the world is a divine vessel:
It cannot be shaped;
Nor can it be insisted upon.
He who shapes it damages it . . . [18]

Act non-action; undertake no undertaking;
taste the tasteless.
The Sage desires the desireless, and
prizes no articles that are difficult
to get.[19]

Many of Lao Tzu's principles become the Tai Chi principles. Many of his teachings influenced or actually became the teachings of the *Tai Chi Classics*.[20] Tai Chi Chuan is the physiological expression of Taoism in the human body. In further illustrating the relationship of Lao Tzu to Tai Chi Chuan let us quote two very pertinent chapters regarding yielding and softness, two essential cornerstones of Tai Chi Chuan.

The weakest things in the world can overmatch
the strongest things in the world.
Nothing in the world can be compared to water
for its weak and yielding nature; yet in attacking
the hard and the strong nothing proves better
than it. For there is no other alternative to it.
The weak can overcome the strong and the yielding
can overcome the hard . . . [21]

• • •

Man when living is soft and tender; when dead he is
hard and tough. All animals and plants when living
are tender and fragile; when dead they become withered
and dry. Therefore it is said: the hard and tough are
parts of death; the soft and tender are parts of life.
This is the reason why the soldiers when they are too
tough cannot carry the day; the tree when it is too
tough will break. The position of the strong and great
is low, and the position of the weak and tender is high.[22]

These principles form the very essence of Tai Chi Chuan and all serious students must strive to imbibe deeply from them.

Spirituality

Using Tai Chi Chuan as a method of advancing one's spiritual development is an idea as old as Tai Chi Chuan itself. As in other forms of spiritual endeavor, progress requires patience, dedication and the continuous practice of correct spiritual disciplines. One's comprehension of the teachings of Tai Chi Chuan must broaden to encompass the idea of Tao—a Supreme Spiritual Substance. One must reinterpret the principles of the *Tai Chi Classics* as a spiritual guide to attain harmony with Tao. Only then will Tai Chi Chuan take on its most spiritual significance. These Principles are as follows:

- Relaxation
- Emptiness and Fullness
- Slowness and Evenness
- Balance
- Rooting and Sinking
- Coordination and Centering
- Breathing
- Concentration

Relaxation

The cardinal principle and rule in Tai Chi Chuan is relaxation. For the serious students of Tai Chi Chuan, this principle must flow through all levels and dimensions of life. We must strive to relax physically, mentally and spiritually. Mental relaxation occurs when we can drop our anxieties and trust in the system of Tai Chi Chuan. Master Cheng Man-ch'ing told us that he first acquired faith in his system of Tai Chi boxing after being challenged by a famous Chinese boxer (Kung Fu expert). Master Cheng said that he really didn't know exactly what happened. He tried to relax as the opponent charged. The next thing he knew, he had evaded the attack and the opponent had been flung into the wall, unconscious. Then for the first time, Master Cheng believed in his Tai Chi Chuan as a martial art. The confidence of faith comes only through experience.

Reading a book on nutrition wil not relieve one's hunger. Merely reading about Tai Chi principles will not bestow the experience. Only through continuous practicing of the principles of Tai Chi Chuan will one gain the required experience.

Relaxation in its highest sense means faith. The greater our faith, the greater our tranquility of mind. Practice faith and gain the experience.

One must have faith in the Tao and that the Tao is benevolent. Once this is established one must learn to relax the self and feel secure in the Tao; having faith that once you surrender to higher forces, the higher forces will take care of you. Trust in Tao, have faith in Tao and Tao will reciprocate ten fold!

Emptiness and Fullness

Both Tai Chi Chuan and Taoist teaching put great emphasis on the idea of becoming empty. When these teachings are interpreted in a spiritual context, emptiness means humility. Humility is the process of seeing oneself in correct perpective to the rest of creation. With such a perspective, one will feel neither proud nor arrogant; nor will he have an unrealistic sense of self-importance.

> Keep empty and you will be filled . . .
> He who has little will receive.
> He who has much will be embarrassed . . .
>
> He does not display himself; therefore he shines.
> He does not approve himself; therefore he is noted
> He does not praise himself; therefore he has merit
> He does not glory in himself; therefore he excels.
> And because he does not compete, therefore no one
> in the world can compete with him. [1]

Taoism extols the virtue of humility and assures the individual who partakes of this teaching, fulfillment.

> He who knows honor and yet keeps to humility
> Will become a valley that receives all the world
> into it . . . [2]

Humility is called "selflessness" in the East. This denotes one who does not regard his own self interests as being more important than anything else. It is also called ego-loss; meaning that the sense of self-importance (of the individual) is gone. It is the opposite of selfishness. Selfishness or egotism, is the idea that one's personal motives should be fulfilled regardless of the consequences to others and to the world. Egotism or selfishness is the main cause of the dangerous and precarious situation of mankind today. It causes class struggle and power plays. It causes man to turn against his fellow man and to take advantage of one another. It arises from the illusion that one's self is the "end-all", that he is autonomous and does not have to answer to anyone or anything.

Selfishness brings greed and destruction. Self-lessness brings love and charity. Feed the self and destroy mankind. Be selfless and the whole world benefits.

> The sage has no self (to call his own);
> He makes the self of the people his self.[3]

> When Tao reigns in the world
> Swift horses are curbed for hauling the dung-carts
> in the field.
> When Tao does not reign in the world
> War horses are bred on the commons outside the city.
> There is no greater crime than seeking what men desire
> There is no greater calamity than indulging in greed . . . [4]

The man grounded in Tao sees himself as but another expression of the Divine. All is Tao. All is sacred and worthy of our reverence and respect.

> To the good I act with goodness;
> To the bad I also act with goodness:
> Thus goodness is attained.[5]

When the Tai Chi Chuan practitioner attains emptiness, he can then become the living channel (way) through which the Tao can flow. Master Cheng would say, "Invest in loss. Little loss little gain, big loss big gain." When we cling tenaciously to our position, or to our concepts of ourselves, we cannot make room for our own growth. It is our ego which prevents us from wanting to lose. Whether this loss is in a push-hands match or the loss of position or prestige, it nevertheless can become our own egotistical stumbling block. This idea is echoed in the great spiritual teachings throughout the world. Jesus taught, "If a man would follow Me, let him renounce the self.[6]" The symbol of Christianity is the cross. One meaning of the symbol is that the personal sense of "I" must be crossed out so that Divinity can manifest. And Buddha taught: "Self is death and truth is life."

Fullness is confidence in the higher spiritual self, and in one's aptitude for nobility, goodness and truth. We must rely on our inner strength, and our ability to transcend the lower impulses. We must have faith in our ultimate destiny to unite with the Tao.

Rooting

Just as a tall building has an unseen foundation which gives it support, Tao is the basic invisible reality which gives essential substance and support to all visible structures in our material world. When Tao becomes our foundation and our root what power can shake us?

Stability and security consist in being rooted in God.[7]

Slowness and Evenness

Just as our Tai Chi form teaches us, spiritual progress must start with the first step and then proceed slowly and continuously. When continuous and sincere action is practiced, success is assured. "Perseverence furthers" states the *I Ching*.

We should seek evenness, not extremes of strictness. Strictness will lead to periods of relative laxness. Thousands of years ago Buddha warned that neither the excesses of ascetisicm not the laxness of self-indulgence would be conducive to spiritual growth. Rather, take the middle path. We must find a norm of living which is within our capabilities and then this norm must slowly be extended and deepened to the more perfected manner of living. Slowness and evenness develop patience and forebearance.

Coordination

Just as one must coordinate all of the physical components of the Tai Chi Form, such as movement, tempo, breathing, relaxation, etc., one must also coordinate one's life in the manner befitting a seeker after Truth. Correct thinking, correct speech and correct action must be incorporated into one's daily life. One must think in a truthful manner. One must not seek to deceive nor should one try to take advantage of others for personal gain. One must practice truthful speech at all times, not gossiping, cursing, or speaking badly of others. One's actions must be in accord with one's thoughts and speech. Noble thoughts and lofty speech are meaningless without proper action. One should think, speak and act Tao.

Tao is found in everything and in all the diverse forms. It is constant and stable. The spiritual aspirant must dwell on this essential unity within divergence and not on the infinite diversity of creation. Diversity will scatter the mind. The essential Oneness will unite it. When this unity is understood, when one realizes that he is intimately connected with his fellow man, then harm to another is understood as being harm to oneself. If the hand should harm the foot because it feels itself separate, then the whole body suffers. The hand does too. One must love himself. This love for one's true self is the basis for service to others. Love expressed through service is probably the singularly most purifying act of spiritual endeavor that one can perform. Service was exemplified by such spiritual giants as Buddha and Christ. Their lives, which were a perfect coordination of thoughts, words and actions, serve as inspiring examples to their fellowmen.

Breathing

Just as breathing is of paramount importance in the physical application of Tai Chi Chuan, so too the breath must take a primary role in the spiritual aspect of Tai Chi. You must begin to identify more and more with your breath. People generally tend to identify with either their bodies or their minds, but we must realize that once the breath enters the nostrils it actually becomes a part of yourself. In fact it becomes a much more important part of yourself than your arms or legs. You can live without your limbs but you cannot live without your breath. Breath is life! One must start to make that association in one's mind and strive to remember this fact.

The breath is also a symbol of something that is more subtle than the gross physical body. It is invisible, ethereal and formless. It symbolizes the Spirit which is in you and around you. As our breath is our life; our spirit is our life. Remove the breath and death is the result; remove the spirit from a body and only a corpse remains. People have the idea that the life within us is unique to ourselves; that my life is different from your life. This is not correct. Life is Spirit. The same spiritual life force permeates and animates all the life forms in the world. What differs is the external containers which hold this spiritual essence. The same electricity gives current to many different bulbs although we may say that the lights are separate and distinct. Another example is a sealed bottle filled with air. The air in the bottle is separated from the air outside. When we uncork the bottle, the air within meets the air without. Where is the separation now? Where does the bottle's air end and the air outside begin? It is the same with the life energy-spirit (Chi) of man. Man feels that his life is separate and distinct from other life around him. But when this life is let out of its container (the body) and merges with the all-pervading Spirit, the sense of individuality dissolves. Just as the air that we breathe is the tangible connection among all beings; spirit is the intangible connection.

Concentration

Meditation

The founders of Tai Chi Chuan were monks who were seeking knowledge of the Self. Meditation was a very important part of their daily spiritual routine. Since the time of its development these monks used Tai Chi as a meditation in movement. But what is meditation and how is Tai Chi used as such?

The word "meditation" comes from the Latin root "media", meaning center. Meditation is the act of turning consciousness towards its own center, so that it perceives itself. When consciousness is able to witness itself, it acquires knowledge of itself. This state is called Self-realization, or enlightenment. Any system of meditation, regardless of its philosophical affiliation, is comprised of three stages: 1. Concentration, 2. Contemplation, and 3. Meditation or Union. One cannot start with stage 3; nor can one decide to skip any stage.

We should also realize that not everyone sitting cross-legged on the floor claiming to meditate is actually meditating. Meditation is a very specific and exact discipline. There is a famous story of a Zen master observing someone sitting cross-legged on the floor. He walked over to him, picked up a stone and started to rub it furiously. Finally the person looked up and inquired about this action. The master answered that he was making a mirror. The person protested that it was impossible to create a mirror by rubbing a stone. The master agreed and added that it was also impossible to achieve enlightenment by merely sitting cross-legged.

Meditation may be further sub-divided into two types; 1. stationary meditation, which is done either in a sitting, kneeling or reclining position (as in the case of sick people). 2. Active meditation, which is done during a specific exercise, during work or while walking.

Before one can even start the actual process of meditation, whether it is stationary or active, one should be aware of certain prerequisites:

1. The spine should be held straight and vertically. This serves two purposes: A) It allows the natural energy system in and around the spinal column to move freely and smoothly up and down the body. B) It helps the body act as an antenna, making it more alert and ready to pick up energy vibrations.

2. The body must be quieted. The mind resides within the body. If the body is in a state of agitation or anxiety, then the mind is also. Meditation seeks to control the mind and to use it as an instrument to probe the inner secrets of consciousness.

3. Breathing must be slow and rhythmic. This allows oxygen to travel to the brain and helps to calm the body.

4. The hands or fingers are arranged in one of several possible postures (called Mudras in Sanscrit). When the hands are so positioned, the positive and negative poles of the body are connected and the electro-magnetic energy of the body is equalized and balanced.[8]

Once these preliminaries are understood, the student is ready to start to meditate. When doing Tai Chi properly, the preliminaries are taken care of by the very structure of the form: the spine is vertical and straight, the body is calm and under control, breathing is coordinated with the slow movements, the hand postures are precise throughout the form, aligning the positive and negative poles.

Stage I—Concentration. As one becomes aware of his mind, one sees that it is like a nervous bundle of thoughts and desires, always wandering and jumping from one topic to the next, often under the control of the senses but rarely under the control of its owner. We must first seek to gain control over the mind's restless state so that it may be directed and harnessed. Concentration (Stage I) is the ability to direct the mind to one subject and to hold it there. Unless this stage is mastered it is useless to talk about further stages. Since ancient times different means of attracting and holding the mind in a state of concentration have been devised by various religions and philosophies. Some systems of meditation teach the visualization of a light or a flame as the focal point for the mind. In Zen meditation, the student is taught to concentrate upon the breath entering and leaving the nostrils, or on the heartbeat. Often the student is advised to study a Zen art such as flower arrangement, archery, or some other martial art to aid the mind in concentrating.[9]

In Tibet, the Mandala is used for concentrating. The Mandala is a circle which is a symbolic depiction of the psyche or self. Often the Buddha is seated in the center of the circle representing the Pure Essence within. The student concentrates on the Mandala until he sees himself. The Tai Chi symbol is also a Mandala. The yin and yang represent the conscious and unconscious aspects of the self.

The Mantra was devised in India, where the science of meditation was scrutinized and elaborated on more fully than in other cultures. A mantra is a sound or group of sounds which the practitioner repeats either verbally or mentally. It is used to gain one-pointedness of mind, and to lead the aspirant to the Self. It has been found that certain sounds are definitely more powerful than others. Studies at Boston University have shown that the repetition of any sound, even "apple pie", can produce the state of concentration and the benefits that accompany it, such as calming of breath, lowering of heartbeat rate, greater relaxation (Alpha state), etc. Other studies have shown that plant and animal life are strongly affected by exposure to sound vibrations. Certain sounds distort and impede the natural growth of plants, while other sounds promote their health and well-being. This is in perfect accord with the teachings of Plato and Pythagoras, both of whom felt that certain ailments could be cured by exposing patients to the correct sounds. Sounds are vibrations. What is the body but vibrating atoms and molecules! The correct vibrations can harmonize the body and the wrong vibrations can create a dissonance. The Indian scriptures teach that the sounds "So Hum", or "Om", or the sound of the name of God are the most powerful mantras available to the spiritual aspirant.

In the Tai Chi Chuan form, the student must first concentrate on learning the moves or postures, then on perfecting them, then on the breathing coordinated with the moves, then on the Chi circulating in the body and Tan Tien, and then on an imaginary opponent. Thus Tai Chi Chuan contains a progressive series of concentration exercises which sharpen the power of concentration. The student of Tai Chi can also benefit from the knowledge and use of mantras. He can choose any mantra he desires and coordinate it with his breathing. For example, So Hum[10]—"So" is coordinated wth each inhalation and "Hum" with every exhalation.

Stage II—Contemplation. Once the student has learned the art of concentrating and is able to hold his mind intently on a chosen subject, he will naturally pass into the second stage called Contemplation. In this stage he loses awareness of himself as the concentrator. He becomes so absorbed in the object of concentration that his center of consciousness shifts to the object itself. He becomes his mantra; he becomes the Tai Chi Form.

Stage III—Meditation (Union). When the practitioner is ripe for the experience, the third stage called Meditation will naturally follow. In this stage the concentrator, the object of concentration and the act of concentration all merge into One. That is, you regain consciousness of yourself concentrating and remain merged in the object of concentration. Union is realized! It expands more and more until one is in a state of mystical union with the entire cosmos. One merges with the Ground of Being, the All, the Ultimate Truth. In this state one transcends the dualities of yin and yang, life and death, and realizes the Oneness of Tao Itself. One attains freedom. This liberation has been called Self-Realization, Cosmic Consciousness, Samadi in Hinduism, Satori in Zen, Nirvana in Buddhism and Heaven in Christianity. Ironically enough, the way to freedom is not by doing whatever one pleases, nor is it chaotic behavior. Rather, it is the way of discipline, effort and self-inquiry. "Forms" (religious, moral, ethical, etc.) are used as tools towards this end. Through the Tai Chi Chuan form, one eventually merges the Chi within himself with the Universal Chi. He experiences Oneness. Once one acquires mastery of a chosen "form" he transcends it through the discipline inherent within that form. For example, a pianist learns a piece of music; he studies it; and later becomes technically excellent. Finally he masters it. At this level he can play the piece brilliantly and simultaneously transcend it by "creating" within the given structure of the music. This is often called "inspiration"—an unconscious surge of creativity. Now the artist is co-creating with the composer of the music and creating an interpretation which is his very own. That is why two great pianists will play the same piece of music and each will move the listener differently. Freedom requires discipline which requires form. One studies a form to attain the Formless. The ultimate aim of Tai Chi Chuan is to transcend the form and reach the Tao.

Tai Chi Chuan
and Other Eastern Systems

Asia is regarded as the cradle of civilization and the fatherland of spiritual world thought. It is not surprising that so many Westerners have turned to the ancient Eastern methods to find comfort and relief from the high paced stress and materiality of the western world. Probably no country better exemplifies a spiritual focus and heritage than does India. India immediately evokes images of holy men and fakirs, industrial backwardness and poverty. It is this strange blend of the exotic and the incomprehensible that fascinates the western mind. Yet, India remains today the same reservoir of spiritual nourishment that it was thousands of years ago when the great Rishies (sages) first wrote down their mystical experiences with the Divine force they encountered in the solitude of mountains and forests, and handed humanity the oldest written spiritual scriptures in order to vouchsafe the prosperity of the world. These ancient writings were named the "Vedas"—wisdom. The Vedas and later scriptures such as Brahmanas, Aranyakas, Upanishads, Ramayana and Mahabarata, comprise a complete philosophical and metaphysical system called Vedanta. It is also correct to call these writings the "science" of spirituality which when diligently adhered to, will lead man from the mundane to the Divine. Science is observation which is verifiable. The precepts of this science of Vedanta were verified by the very lives of its authors and can be further corroborated by anyone wishing to test their validity by following these inspired prescriptions. Vedanta is divided into six main systems of knowledge. Yoga is one of the six orthodox systems. Somewhere between the first and second century B.C., the great Rishi Pantanjali formulated his *Yoga Sutras* which was the first written compilation of Yoga, the holy science.

Tai Chi Chuan and Yoga

The word "Yoga" means "union". The aim of yoga is the union of man with Brahman. Brahman is defined as something which has no discernible dimensions and which is limitless (similar to the Chinese definition of Tao). The term Yoga can also mean a particular system or method of self-discipline used to gain mastery over the self (similar to the Chinese term "Kung Fu"). Tai Chi Chuan, when comprehended in its highest term, means the supreme ultimate system of self-discipline which leads one to union with Tao. In speaking of Yoga we can divide our discussion into two distinct aspects, the philosophical system called Hinduism and the physical system of body exercise called "Hatha Yoga".

To adequately discuss the philosophical similarities and differences between the Chinese and Indian systems could take a book in itself. I will briefly mention some outstanding points which may prove of interest to the Tai Chi Chuan student. Yoga is one of many paths of knowledge in Hinduism. Hatha Yoga is one branch of Yoga but there are many other important branches i.e. Raja Yoga (mind), Karma Yoga (Action-Work), Bakti Yoga (Love-Devotion), Jhani Yoga (Wisdom), etc. All are paths to the Divine Union. The original unmanifested Reality which is termed "Tao" by the Taoist is termed "Brahman" by the Hindus. The concept of Yin and Yang is expressed as "Shiva-Shakti" which stands for duality and the male and female principles. This duality is also expressed as "Bramanda and Pindanda" or "Paramatma and Jivatma" meaning the Universal and the individual. This duality is inherent in the emanated creation which has Brahman as its Creator and as its One and Only Core Reality.

The *I Ching* states:

> These two cardinal principles of all existence are then symbolized in the two fundamental hexagrams of the *Book of Changes*, THE CREATIVE and THE RECEPTIVE. In the last analysis, this cannot be called a dualism. The two principles are united by a relation based on homogeneity.[1]

Yoga teaches that all such dualities and individualties are only "relatively real" since they are in a constant state of change and therefore impermanent. This is also expressed in the *I Ching*:

> Nonchange is the background, as it were, against which change is made possible. For in regard to any change there must be some fixed point to which the change can be referred.[2]

> In the philosophy of the *Book of Changes* nothing is regarded as being absolutely at rest; rest is merely an intermediate state of movement, latent movement.[3]

Dualities are a product of "Maya" (illusion caused by the mind's preferences and prejudices). The mind sees the division but fails to see the unity. It becomes man's destiny to realize Brahman and to evolve from the "lower self"—the individual—to the "higher self"—the Divine, the spark of Brahman contained in all (called the "Atma"). Once the Atma is realized as man's essential reality, man will penetrate the veil of Maya and realize the Unity within the diversity. The Atma unites with Paramatma—the Spirit in man unites with the Universal Spirit and Yoga (Union) is realized.

Hatha Yoga is a system of preparing and purifying the physical body in order to create a better vehicle with which to gain the realization of Brahman. The physical similarities between Hatha Yoga and Tai Chi Chuan are striking. In fact Tai Chi Chuan is sometimes referred to as Chinese Yoga. Both systems emphasize breath energy called "Prana" or "Chi" respectively. Both are physical exercises demanding great concentration on choreographed postures which require relaxation and coordinated breathing. In fact one particular yogic exercise called "the salutation to the sun" is performed like Tai Chi Chuan, that is, it strings a series of postures (asanas) together in a particularly flowing and continuous sequence. However, in the practice of most yogic asanas there is a noticeable difference from Tai Chi. Hatha Yoga has many static postures and there are slight rest periods in between one posture and another. These rests are required because the body has been taxed by the nature of holding the particular posture. Tai Chi Chuan is continuous and the body does not need to rest because postures flow too quickly to tire the body. Hatha Yoga has breathing exercises which are practiced independently of body movements. This is not true in Tai Chi. In Tai Chi the energy is circulated up the front of the body and down the back of the body following the meridians of Chinese medicine (that is, accupuncture meridians). In Hatha Yoga the energy is raised up the spinal column through seven Chakras (spinning wheels of energy) until the energy finally becomes centered in the Crown Chakra (Sagasrara) located at the top of the head. In Tai Chi the aim is to center and store the energy in the Tan Tien (located about two inches below the navel). The chakra which corresponds to the Tan Tien is called the Swadhistana Chakra in the Indian system. A fascinating fact is that although two different chakras are emphasized in the two systems, Yoga teaches that these two chakras are vitally connected and that concentration on the Swadhistana (Tan Tien) can activate this connection and raise the energy directly to the Crown Chakra (Sagasrara).

Mastery of either system has produced people with super-normal powers called "siddhis" in Yoga, and Kung Mastery in Chinese. Both emphasize breath energy, concentration, relaxation and willpower. Both ultimately teach that in order to excel, surrender (wu wei) is essential. The path of Yoga which emphasizes surrender is called Bakti Yoga. Bakti Yoga is the path of love, faith and surrender. Surrender in either system requires faith in something worthy, a Benevolent Power which will foster and protect. This power is called Brahman in Yoga, Tao in Tai Chi Chuan and God in the West. Faith requires experience. To acquire the experience one must practice the prescribed life. Live the life and know the Truth!

Zen

The Japanese word "Zen" is derived from the Chinese word "Chan" which means meditation. Chan meditation was imported into China along with Buddhism from India, and was derived from the Indian meditation called "Dhyana".

Zen Buddhism has its roots in Indian Buddhism and picked up much of the Chinese Taoist influence. Zen regards Buddidharma (Ta-mo) as its founder, and places heavy emphasis on meditation. The goal of Zen is enlightenment or Self-realization, but aside from these things the similarities to the original Buddhism end. Zen does not follow any of the Buddha's moral teachings or precepts. It is amoral, that is, it does not concern itself with morality per se. It is neither theistic nor nihilistic. It is not concerned with the profound philosophical revelations of Buddha, such as the Law of Karma, or Reincarnation. It has a great mistrust of books, lectures, and organized systems. Zen is the purest existential experience of the now. The present is the only reality. Zen professes that enlightenment is imminently possible at any moment in one's life. One must strive to be attentive to the opportunities that are everywhere manifesting and to tune into the omnipresent truth that underlies all of life. The sight of a bird flying, the sound of a brook bubbling, a bell ringing, or the fragrance of a flower in a field, all of these, and an infinite variety of other things, may bring the transcendental experience of reality to the awareness of the seeker. The only obstacle to the perception of this reality is man's own mind with its confused and distorted perceptions. Thus the state called "no-mind" is sought. No-mind is a meditative state in which man can cut through the illusions of life and perceive Truth. To attain this state several things are helpful. An enlightened teacher can be an invaluable aid as he can perceive your illusions and help you to cut through them more quickly. Usually he will advise ZaZen (Zen meditation) and a Koan.

ZaZen places great emphasis on the breath called Ki (Chi). The student will sit and follow the breath from the nose to the Hara (Tan Tien), taking painstaking care to time the inhalation and exhalation exactly. In this respect ZaZen parallels Tai Chi Chuan which emphasizes the exact execution of the breathing coordinated to each and every posture of the form. A second type of meditation is called Walking Meditation in which the Zen student merely walks slowly and deliberately, paying particular attention to his balance, breathing and Hara.[4] This illustrates most dramatically the similarity to Tai Chi Chuan.

A Koan is a device for self-inquiry. It is a question given by one's Zen Master to bring the mind to such a state of agitation that it will have no choice but to transcend itself. A typical Koan is: What was your face like before your parents were born? Or, what is the sound of one hand clapping? These Koans are asked in total seriousness and demand answers. Eventually after much struggle, the answer comes, not through the thought process which is inadequate to the task but rather it comes through the intuition when a mighty surge of unconscious energy finally bursts forth after much agonizing frustration. The answer does not come in words but as an experience of the reality of life. The original face sought after is the original nature of man (Tao). This nature cannot be grasped intellectually but must be experienced. Once the experience is had, one knows himself and his relationship to the rest of life. In Japanese the words "shoga" and "daiga" are used to differentiate between the smaller self, and the greater self. The aim of Zen is to cut through the illusion that the body or mind (shoga) is the self and to perceive the daiga as the true self—the original nature. This true nature is often referred to as "Mu". Mu is emptiness which is at the same time saturated, very similar to the definition given to Tao. In fact the similarities to Taoism are more striking than to Buddhism. In Zen as in Taoism, Buddhism or Yoga, the goal is the same—to experience the True Self which is an indefinable spiritual substance. It is both full and empty because it is essence without form. Yet it is in all forms just as clay is inherent in pottery of all shapes. Zen often uses ceremonies or art forms as tools to perceive this essential reality contained within these forms. These are termed the "Zen Arts". Typical are the tea ceremony, gardening and the martial arts. In Japan to study a martial art without the Zen aspect is to miss the essence of the art. Therefore, the great Japanese martial artists of Bushido (sword), Archery, Karate, Judo, Aikido, etc., use their arts as the primary vehicle to discover the nature of the True Self, as did the original monks who founded Shaolin and Tai Chi Chuan.

Years ago when I was a student of Korean Karate (Yun Mu Kuan), my instructor, Master Min Pai, told me that if I wanted to advance my art further, it would now be necessary to study ZaZen and he advised me to study with his own Zen master, Yasutani Roshi, who at that time was considered one of the most enlightened masters of the Rienzi sect. I was taught a meditation technique which involved concentration on my breathing and on lowering my mind to a point about two inches below the navel (Tan Tien). For many months I diligently persevered until one evening as I was sitting serenely in practice, I was able to clearly see my consciousness descending from the region of my head and moving downward with each breath until it reached the point that I had set months earlier as my goal. The instant that my mind reached the Tan Tien I experienced a blinding flash of light and energy in my head. I seemed transported to a region beyond time and space. Time stopped and I became aware of each and every cell in my body being bathed in ecstatic currents of energy. I became very aware of the unity of energy that connected all the cells and made them one. I could not identify my mind or my body as being separate from this energy. The question of the relationship between body and mind is, of course, an ancient one. In Zen, it is promptly resolved by the statement, "the mind and body are one". That experience dwarfed all of my previous experiences of sensation and pleasure. Sexual ecstasy was paled by comparison. I'm sure that if someone were timing that experience they would have said that it lasted only a few seconds. But subjectively speaking, I entered a state that seemed eternal. I realized that this was the deepest and most fulfilling experience of my life and that my new goal would now be to recapture that state. I also realized that any effort or sacrifice necessary on my part to regain this state would certanly be well worth it. For this reason Zen holds a very dear place in my mind and I shall always feel indebted to its practice. Zen helped open up psychic and spiritual channels in my life and as a result I was inspired to go on to study with many other great masters of both the East and the West. This culminated with the meeting of my present Spiritual Master, Sathya Sai Baba who is Knowledge, Love, Compassion and Bliss personified.

Tai Chi Chuan and Western Psychology

In the West we use the word psychology to mean the study of the mind. As I have already stated in the definition, Tai Chi Chuan is a mental discipline. Anyone familiar with the teachings of Western psychology and with the teachings of Tai Chi can make some very striking analogies and comparisons between these two systems, which are so different in origin. If we start examining some of the most prevalent theories concerning learning, and the workings and structure of the psyche in Western psychology, we will see that these concepts have long been incorporated into the system of Tai Chi Chuan.

Western psychology is prepared to offer many theories ranging from the most scientific to the mystical, to explain how knowledge is acquired by man. These theories can be broadly categorized under two main sub-divisions.

1. B.F. Skinner, who is a behaviorist, states that knowledge is acquired from the outside physical universe via the senses. It can be modified by conditioning.

2. Carl Jung, and probably the majority of contemporary psychologists, feel that knowledge comes from a combination of outside stimuli and from inside a man via unconscious, archetypal experiences either genetically inherited or from knowledge acquired from previous lives.

Tai Chi Chuan is an ancient Chinese method of acquiring knowledge and wisdom. This method incorporates both of the above Western concepts. We can call it a "consciousness expanding form", because one cannot practice Tai Chi Chuan without increasing conscious awareness of one's body and one's self. It deliberately and systematically changes one's perception of the self and the relationship between the self and the world. One must practice the slow motion, dance-like movements several times daily and keep these points always in mind:

- To be as totally relaxed as possible.
- To synchronize the breathing with each movement of the form.
- To keep the speed constant and fluid.
- To align the spine vertically for optimum balance and strength.
- To move the entire body as one unit with no isolated sections moving independently.

- To concentrate on a mental image of an opponent attacking and defending.
- To concentrate on the cultivation of Chi throughout the body.

Concentration is focused on the body for long intervals of uninterrupted time while practicing the form. As one tries to relax and keep all of the above mentioned in mind, one begins to notice that there is tension in this shoulder or that joint: this knee is not bent and that elbow is. Then one changes incorrect practice, that is, external body tension, which is a symptom of internal mental tension. The body and mind learn to be more relaxed and calm. Thus, Tai Chi Chuan has been employing Skinnerian methods of "behavior modification" thousands of years before Skinner.

Jung had an altogether different concept of man's psyche. He was able to portray this as a diagram of a cross within the circle. The cross is an ancient symbol of consciousness and the circle is the Eastern mandala which represents the psyche.

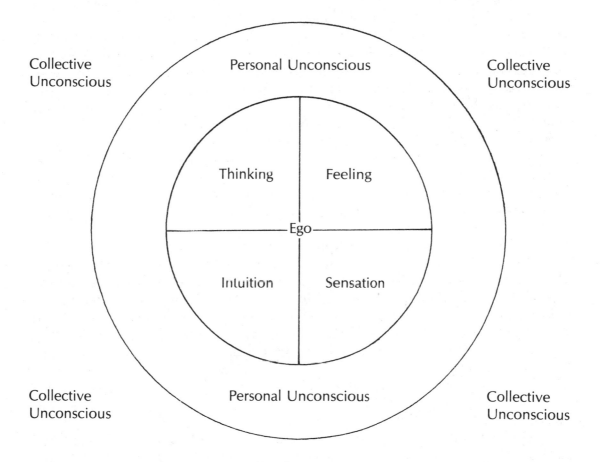

According to Jung, all knowledge goes to the center of the cross, the ego or spirit. The ego itself actually does nothing other than observe; it can be likened to the Atma (Spirit) of Hinduism, the consciousness within man that is the Eternal Witness. The ego is fed information via the four functions of consciousness: thinking, feeling, sensation, and intuition. If we look closely at sensation we see that Jung meant the physical body with its panorama of nerves and sensory equipment. Thinking also stems from the body, that is, the brain. Both these functions, thinking and sensation, are called rational functions and they constitute a minor portion of Jung's overall scheme. The remaining two, feeling and intuition, are termed irrational. Surrounding these four functions we see a layer of unconsciousness, borrowed from Freud, called the Personal Unconscious. This is the area where all those recorded tid-bits, which we have forgotten, are stored. They can be brought back to consciousness by such techniques as hypnosis, psycho-analysis, etc. Surrounding the entire diagram, Jung places the Collective Unconscious as a sort of sea in which every human being's psyche is sustained. This Collective Unconscious contains all the collected knowledge and energy of mankind, including all man's patterns and archetypes. This knowledge can be tapped and explored by such means as meditation, psychedelic drugs, E.S.P., or dreams, or it may stream forth via the intuition under the conditions of stress or during psychotic episodes. This then, is the wisdom of the sages; the remembered knowledge of Plato, and the Kenso and Satori experience of Zen. Jung felt that all four functions, thinking, feeling, sensation, and intuition have to be nurtured in order to supply knowledge to the ego and extend man's conscious mind.[1]

Chi, also, is unconscious energy. In Jung's psychological context, the Collective Unconscious is an ever-present knowledge available to all, but which remains unconscious to most. Tai Chi cultivates Chi from within. Chi is "life energy". Chi strengthens and sustains life. It is present everywhere and has existed from the creation of the primary manifestation (the Tai Chi). It contains within itself the seed of our lives, and the source of our wisdom. Life energy (Chi) is the energy of consciousness.

To deepen one's experience of Chi is to deepen one's experience of life and to expand one's consciousness—this is the acquisition of true wisdom. That is why it is said that the Tai Chi master acquires the wisdom of a sage and the knowledge of Tao.

Dr. Robert E. Ornstein, psychologist, has done an admirable job of assimilating Western psychology, the more scientific and objective approach to understanding the self, with the Eastern introspective and subjective approach. In his book, The Psychology of Consciousness,[2] Dr. Ornstein explores with considerable depth the subject of the two sides of the brain. He points out that as early as 1864 the neurologist, Hughling Jackson, considered the left hemisphere to be the seat of the "faculty of expression". It is concerned with analytic, logical thinking, especially in verbal and mathematical functions. It underlies logical thought, language and mathematics. The right hemisphere is primarily responsible for our spatial orientation, artistic endeavors, crafts and image recognition.

It is noted that most people tend to rely more heavily on either the right or the left hemisphere in their daily lives, that is, the analytic professor as compared with the artist or the craftsman.

The two hemispheres of the brain form the basis of the polarity that has touched much of Western psychology. Examples of these are the "conscious and the subconscious" of Freud, and the "introvert and extrovert" of Jung. Ornstein sees this polarity as being the same as the duality that is expressed in Vedanta between the intellect (Buddhi) and the mind (Manas), and the Chinese concept of yin and yang.

As we reflect on Ornstein's discussion of the two hemispheres of the brain we can better understand why Tai Chi Chuan is translated as a Supreme Ultimate System of body and mind development. Tai Chi utilizes both sides of the brain.

Obviously the practice of the Tai Chi form involves aesthetic and artistic movements which must stimulate and exercise the right hemisphere of the brain. It is equally obvious that the sequential arrangement of the Tai Chi form, with its intrinsic conceptual exercises, must also provide equal stimulation for the left hemisphere of the brain. It is also interesting to note how various postures in the Tai Chi form are more conspicuously performed on either the right or left side of the body. The body's weight is also constantly shifting from the left to the right side. This not only stimulates the left and right hemispheres of the brain, but the left and right meridian channels of energy as depicted on acupuncture charts. This establishes a physical and a psychic balance throughout the the entire organism.

In Tai Chi Chuan one is taught to concentrate on an imaginary fighting opponent and to practice relaxing in front of this rival. In contemporary psychology, Joseph Wolpe's "Systematic Desensitization"[3] teaches the very same thing. Wolpe instructed his patients to relax their muscles while imagining scenes that caused anxiety. Then, when the real life situation occurred, it was much less stressful.

The current trend in psychology to use sensitivity training to increase awareness has its parallel in the Tai Chi exercise called "Push Hands". While practicing this exercise, two people become sensitive to each other's energy through constant tactile contact. This also increases awareness of one's self and of one's own internal energy flow.

There is one other system of psychology that should be mentioned. William Reich's theory of Orgone Energy.[4] Reich maintains that Orgone Energy is an all-pervading energy available to everyone. It is life energy; it is sexual energy; it is psychic energy. Contact with this energy is vital for one's well-being. The energy is most easily experienced during a sexual orgasm, although it is by no means limited to sex. People, during the course of their development, block the natural accesibility to this energy by tensions and anxieties in their bodies and minds. One method of curing this condition called "armoring" is to massage the body in a very specific manner which makes up part of Reichian Therapy. It is interesting that Reich's description of Orgone Energy is so similar to the definitions of Chi, and that the elimination of tension in the body is necessary to both systems.

Tai Chi Chuan can be outlined in terms of Western psychology as follows:

1. Physical: form study, push hands—(Skinner)
2. Mental: Concentration, sixth sense development, Chi—(Jung, Wolpe)
3. Unconscious Energy: Chi—(Jung, Reich)
4. Spiritual: Meditation in movement, Chi, Cosmic Consciousness—(Jung)

Tai Chi masters of the past attained notable insight into all four of these levels. They developed extraordinary powers and strength. Their feats have become Chinese legends and folklore. Their wisdom has served as an inspiration for millions. The philosophy that they lived—yield before an adversary or obstacle, never resist or become tense—endures as a teaching and guide that few can rationally oppose. Nature itself illustrates this principle for us when mighty oaks fall where reeds withstand the storms.

Tai Chi Chuan and Occult Systems

The word "occult" means hidden. Occult knowledge, therefore, is a body of knowledge and practices hidden or veiled from the general mass of people. To gain this knowledge one must arduously proceed step by step within a given structured system from the initiate to the adept. This requires discipline. All systems of Kung Fu may be considered occult systems of ancient China. All occult systems are ultimately venturing in different ways to accomplish the same end—knowledge of the Self. The Tai Chi Chuan student should understand that Tai Chi Chuan is not an isolated phenomenon, rather it is part of a much greater body of occult knowledge, comprised of many different systems. Symbolism and methodology are often shared in common, although they may be explained differently. The occult sciences most frequently practiced in the West, are called the Hermetic Sciences and are those attributed to Throth Hermes Trismegistus,[1] an Egyptian who was called "Thrice Greatest" because he was considered greatest in philosophy, greatest of priests and greatest of kings. He was also called "Messenger of God" and considered the embodiment of wisdom. These Hermetic Sciences include the Kabala, Alchemy, Astrology, Tarot and Magic. When we speak of western occultism, we usually refer to one of the above five systems. All of these systems represent deep psychological systems of inquiry into the nature of man and man's relationship to God and to the rest of the cosmos. Thus the letters of the Hebrew alphabet (Kabala), the alchemical terms, the pictures of the Tarot deck, the good and evil spirits of magic were all symbols to explain the self and the nature of reality to the initiated. P.D. Ouspensky, philosopher, psychologist, mystic and scholar writes:

> But when the true alchemist spoke of seeking for gold, he spoke of gold in the soul of man. And he called gold that which in the New Testament is called the Kingdom of Heaven, and in Buddhism, Nirvana. And when the true astrologer spoke of constellations and planets he spoke of constellations and planets in the soul of man, i.e., of the qualities of the human soul, and its relations to God and to the world. And when the true Kabalist spoke of the Name of God, he sought this Name in the soul of man and in Nature, not in dead books, nor in biblical texts, as did the Kabalist-Scholastics. The Kabala, Alchemy, Astrology, and Magic are parallel symbolical systems of psychology and metaphysics.[2]

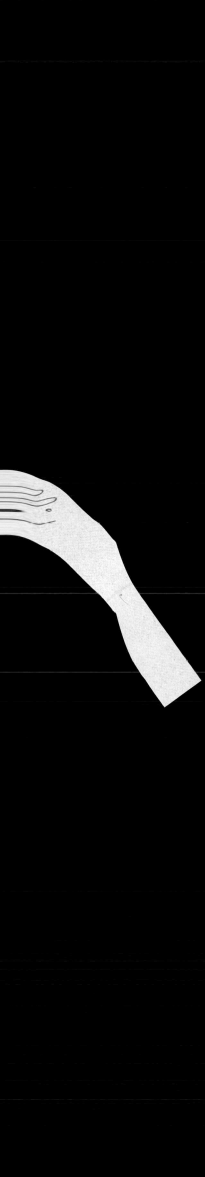

In Ceremonial Magic there are many rites and rituals which may be compared to Tai Chi Chuan. For example: in order to perform a ritual, one "casts" a circle or square, which is a particular space exclusively set apart from everywhere else. In Tai Chi Chuan we may think of the specific area set aside for the performance of the form as this space. Don Juan, the Yaki Indian Brujo (sorcerer) in Castenada's *Tales of Power*, teaches Casteneda about "power spots" which are geographical locations where one is exceptionally secure and powerful. The Brujo apprentice also learns a "power dance" for self-protection. The Tai Chi form has been termed "the deadly dance" because to perform it absolutely correctly is to grasp all its principles and thus be invincible. An even more profound interpretation of the "power spot" is the Tan Tien, located just below the navel. This spot accumulates Chi and controls our center of balance and our center of energy. In tarot card readings, astrology, or in crystal gazing the reader must be aware of this center of power within himself from which all projections and perceptions emanate. He knows that since the center is within himself, he alone must assume responsibility for all he perceives. In Tarot and in Astrology the practitioner is constantly dwelling on the union and the relative relationship of all creation as is reflected in his art.

In Ceremonial Magic, a given ceremony starts with the practitioner facing each of the four primary directions and invoking assistance from the power inherent in each. In Tai Chi Chuan one also starts by facing one of the primary directions and performs a type of ceremony (The Opening), he then proceeds to the other directions. Parallel analogies are found in Kabala in the four letters of the name of God: I.H.V.H.; in alchemy in the four elements: fire, water, air and earth; and in the tarot in the four suits: wands, cups, swords and pentacles. The two colors of the tarot deck (red and black) symbolize the binary which is expressed as yin and yang in Tai Chi. Wand and sword express activity of consciousness (yang); cups and pentacles express passivity (yin).

The four elements of Western Alchemy: Fire, Water, Earth, and Air correspond to the four elements of Chinese alchemy: Fire, Water, Earth and Metal respectively. To these four, the Chinese added one more element, Wood. Wood symbolizes the Spirit or LIfe Force. When the Life Force is added to the four elements we get "Wu Hing"—the five Chinese elements, symbolized by the Pentagram, the symbol of man.

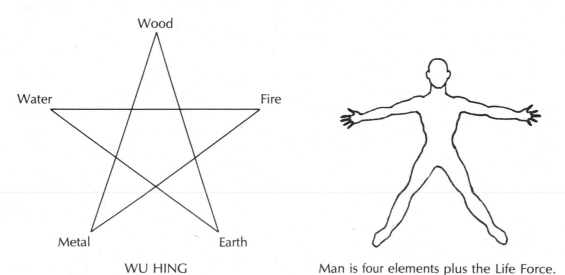

WU HING   Man is four elements plus the Life Force.

According to Chinese (Taoist) philosophy, the five elements came forth from the Tai Chi. The interplay of these five elements produced everything in the Universe. The five elements were applied to many things in ancient Chinese life.

	Wood	Fire	Earth	Metal	Water
Tai Chi Posture—	Retreat	Gaze Right	Central Equilib.	Advance	Look Left
Colors—	Green	Red	Yellow	White	Black
Direction—	East	South	Center	West	North
Flavor—	Sour	Bitter	Sweet	Pungent	Salty
Season—	Spring	Summer	Late Summ.	Autumn	Winter
Sense—	Vision	Speech	Taste	Smell	Hearing
Martial Arts—	Staff	Spear	Hands	Knife	Sword
Planets—	Jupiter ♃	Mars ♂	Saturn ♄	Venus ♀	Mercury ☿
Emotions—	Anger	Joy	Sympathy	Grief	Fear

In all of the above systems, as in Tai Chi Chuan, the communion with Higher Powers within and without one's self (Universal Energy—Chi, God—Tao) is sought through visualization, concentration, repetition and willpower. When concentration and repetition are practiced, willpower is increased and one becomes master over himself and his environment. The goal of the occult is to become a channel for Universal Energy.

In fact the transmission of this energy by touch from the teacher (healer) to the student (patient) is common in occult tradition. It is called "laying on of hands" and it is used in training processes, healing and in graduation ceremonies. This tradition also applies to martial arts. The teacher spars with the student. What is actually taking place is more than just sparring practice; it is a subtle transference of energy from the greater to the lower. Only in this manner can the student truly advance. In Tai Chi the "push hands" exercise replaces conventional sparring. The student learns from the touch of the master. One could attempt to describe the correct push or neutralization technique but it is only through experiencing the touch from the master that the concept can be grasped. This non-verbal communication is absolutely essential if the student wishes to approach the teacher's level. For this reason the teacher in Tai Chi, as in other occult practices, is indispensible. Once the student acquires adeptness, it then becomes his responsibility to use his skill selflessly.

My Tai Chi Chuan master, Cheng Man-ch'ing, was aware of this important end and was himself ceaselessly engaged in healing patients that would come to him for help. He understood that the highest possible use of one's energy (Chi) is to help others. We, too, should seek to use our energy to heal and to help ourselves and others.

Tai Chi Chuan and Health

Tai Chi Chuan is the most popular martial art in the world. This is primarily because of its health benefits. What are these benefits? How does Tai Chi improve health? What illnesses does Tai Chi affect?

Both Tai Chi Chuan and Chinese Medicine are outgrowths of Taoism. It is, therefore, no wonder that both of these systems are in such harmony and alignment with one another and that they compliment each other so perfectly. There is a legendary claim that Tai Chi Chuan can ward off 640 different ailments. This claim, however, has yet to be supported by modern medicine. Some of the ailments that Tai Chi Chuan is reputed to help are:

Arteriosclerosis	Insomnia
Arthritis	Kidney Malfunctions
Asthma	Lethargy
Bronchitis	Liver Disease
Cholecystitis	Loss of Breath
Colds	Low Blood Pressure
Constipation	Nervous Disorders
Diabetes	Neurasthenia
Dizziness	Paralysis
Flus	Rheumatism
Gastrointestinal Disorders	Senility
Heart Disease	Stress
Hemiparesis	Tuberculosis
High Blood Pressure	Ulcers
Hypertension	

My teacher Master Cheng Man-ch'ing was a famous doctor and professor of Chinese Medicine. He directed countless patients to take up the practice of Tai Chi Chuan as part of their medical treatment. He prescribed it to strengthen their bodies and to prevent relapses. He was a great believer in Tai Chi as a preventive as well as a curative treatment for illnesses. He himself was cured of tuberculosis after diligent prac-

59

tice of Tai Chi. I personally know two other Tai Chi teachers who make similar claims of cures to themselves through Tai Chi Chuan, Master T.T. Liang and Benjamin Lo. In addition to these three distinguished and reputable Tai Chi instructors, I can state that many of my own students have come to me innumerable times after class to inform me of how their particular physical problems have been clearing up since practicing Tai Chi Chuan. My own general health has improved noticeably since studying Tai Chi. Whereas I used to contract about five severe colds per year, I have had approximately that same number of colds in total, over the last fifteen years.

In order to understand exactly how Tai Chi Chuan improves health, one must have an understanding of the Five Elements, Chinese Medicine, the meridian system and the concept of Chi.

Both Chinese Medicine and Tai Chi Chuan are rooted in Taoism and the theory of yin and yang. Man is the microcosm (yin) and the Universe is the macrocosm (yang). The yin and yang components must be kept in harmony in order for peace and prosperity to exist. The human body also is divided into binaries of yin and yang components which should be in relative equilibrium if good health is to be maintained. These yin and yang binaries are innately present in the positions of the body (i.e. the top and bottom, front and back, etc.), in the organs, and in the energy components (positive and negative electrical charges). An even balance of yin and yang energy ensures good health. But if this energy is disturbed or displaced in one direction or another, for example, by eating poorly, by inhaling foul air, by not exercising properly, by excessive heat or cold, anger or fear, etc., a type of "short circuit" in the body's energy occurs manifesting as pain or some other negative symptom. If these symptoms are not heeded and if the energy imbalance is not corrected it will in turn lead to poor health, disease and finally death. Thus, illness is defined, in Chinese Medicine, as an imbalanced or inadequate circulation of body energy—Chi. Chinese Medicine is based upon the theory that Chi circulates through very fine channels or pathways called "Ching" or meridians. Normally in a 24 hour period, Chi will circulate twice throughout the meridians of the body. A disturbance of the body's energy equilibrium will be reflected in one or more of these meridians. Any disturbance of the energy flow within a meridian will manifest as pain or some disorder.

Actually the idea of energy traveling through the body was not unique to China. The Vedas, which are the oldest spiritual texts, are the basis of an ancient Indian system of medicine called "Avedic Medicine". Avedic Medicine's teachings include the circulation of physical and spiritual energy (Prana) within the body. For example, it identifies three energy passages in the spine, which are called the Ida, the Pingala and the Sushumna. The Ida and Pingala are the two outer passages of the spinal cord, the Sushumna is the central passage. The Hindu concepts of energy flow, however, were never as specifically and precisely charted with corresponding surface points as in the Chinese system.

How the exact points were originally mapped out and determined is not exactly known. Some believe that the correspondence of certain points to specific organs was first determined on the battlefields when treating the wounded. Others believe that it was the meticulous observation of certain highly sensitive points on the body by doctors and healers over hundreds of years. Another theory holds that early forms of "bleeding" of patients intended to remove bad blood, resulted in the observation that certain points, when punctured, lead to the immediate relief of pain. Still another theory states that these points were actually visible to certain "seers" or highly psychic individuals, just as certain people today can see auras (the energy field surrounding the body). These people mapped out the radiant spots of energy that they saw and later proceeded to experiment with the points that they had plotted. These points became the acupuncture points which are used today. Whatever its origin, acupuncture today remains a science as complex as any system of internal medicine in the West.

When dissection was first practiced in China (about 1000 A.D.), the meridians could not be seen to have any physical existence yet the proof of their existence was inferred by the effect that was exerted on the organs and on the body in general. Today, acupuncture points can be detected by sophisticated electrically sensitive apparatus and also by the use of Kirlian photography.[1] Meridians have their origin in specific organs; an organ is defined (in Chinese Medicine) as a "functioning system". The twelve main meridians are: Lungs, Large Intestine, Stomach, Spleen, Triple-Heater, Heart-Constrictor, Small Intestine, Gall-Bladder, Heart, Liver, Kidney and Bladder. The Triple-Heater meridian controls the energy of respiration, the internal temperature of the organs, the distribution of the energy to the uro-genital organs and the energy of the sex drive. The Heart-Constrictor meridian controls the energy of the circulatory system and blood vessels through to the filtering portions of the kidneys, and is also related to sexual energy.

Meridians can also be looked at as a direct link between the internal organs and the outside environment via the acupuncture points on the skin surface.

The Five Elements - Wu Hing

Chinese philosophy divides the world into five elements: Wood, Fire, Earth, Metal and Water. These elements are symbolic and represent five forces in nature. The constant interplay between these five forces constitutes the structure and the make-up of creation. The first element is Wood. It represents the life force or spirit, which is responsible for the growth of living organisms in nature (such as trees). This formless life force is usually concealed from our sight by its form, which is wood, its material structure. Wood burns and gives rise to Fire. From fire comes ashes—Earth. Earth gives rise to Metal. Metal (called "Air" in western occult philosophy) is a mineral. Plants need minerals (as well as air) for their growth. Therefore, minerals give rise to Wood, and the cycle is constantly replenishing and renewing itself. This is the creative interplay of the five elements (Seng cycle). The five elements also interplay destructively, meaning they break down creation. Disintegration is necessary before regeneration can occur. Therefore, disintegration and generation are but two aspects of the same process (yin and yang). The destructive interplay (Ko cycle) is as follows:

Wood destroys Earth—plants break up rocks and soil, ancient wooden plows tilled the soil.
Earth destroys Water—earth absorbs water, earth impedes the natural flow of water.
Water destroys Fire—water extinguishes fire.
Fire destroys Metal—fire melts metal
Metal destroys Wood—metal cuts wood.

The laws of the five elements take on great significance to health when applied to the organs and meridians of the body.

		Yin	Yang
Wood——	Liver		Gall Bladder
Fire——	Heart		Small Intestine
Earth——	Spleen		Stomach
Metal——	Lung		Large Intestine
Water——	Kidney		Bladder
Fire——	Heart-Constrictor		Triple-Heater

If we apply the law of the interplay of the five elements we find that when we stimulate the Kidney meridian (Water), the Liver (Wood) will also be stimulated because water creates wood. Also the Heart (Fire) will be sedated because water destroys fire. In like manner, all of the meridians interact with one another according to their elemental relationship as depicted in the pentagram figure. One can therefore see the importance of understanding the laws of the five elements before starting to apply treatment to any of the meridians. Certainly anyone interested in acupuncture must familiarize himself thoroughly with the five elements, their corresponding meridians, and the laws that govern their interplay.

Diagnosing

Chinese Medicine uses three main means of diagnosing the energy imbalance in the body:

1. *Pulse diagnosis on the wrists.* The twelve meridians are reflected in three pairs of pulses on each wrist. The relative differences as registered on the pulses of the two wrists will reveal the energy balance or imbalance within the entire body.

Left Wrist (yang)		Right wrist (yin)	
yang—	Small Intestine	yang—	Large Intestine
yin—	Heart	yin—	Lungs
yang—	Gall-Bladder	yang—	Stomach
yin—	Liver	yin—	Spleen
yang—	Bladder	yang—	Triple-Heater
yin—	Kidneys	yin—	Heart-Constrictor

2. *Abdominal diagnosis.* The abdomen is examined for surface temperature, softness or firmness, palpitation and any type of pain which will reflect meridian energy imbalance.

3. *Body observation.* Particularly the face, voice, skin tone, lines, and color.

By a combination of these three main methods, doctors of Chinese Medicine can ascertain if an energy imbalance exists in a person. When an imbalance is detected it is generally treated in one of several ways.

Treatments

The treatments are: 1. Acupuncture, 2. Moxibustion, 3. Herbs, 4. Massage, 5. Diet, 6. Physical and breathing exercises. Any or all of the above methods may be successfully employed to reestablish the correct balance of yin and yang distribution within the body. The first three methods are considered faster-acting and are more radical changes to the body. Acupuncture is the most radical of the methods. The remaining treatments are more subtle and generally take longer periods of time in order to show the effect that they are inducing. In certain situations one method is acceptable and another is not. For example, certain acupuncture points should never be needled and certain points should never have moxibustion. In other situations any one of the above six methods may be perfectly acceptable. Often several of the methods are employed simultaneously. Such decisions, therefore, must be left up to the expertise of a competent doctor.

1. **Acupuncture.** The earliest known document on Chinese Medicine is the *Nei Ching* or *Classic of Internal Medicine* attributed to Huang Ti—The Yellow Emperor (2697–2596 B.C.) This work also included the first written text on Chinese acupuncture. It was not until the seventeenth century that Jesuit missionaries returning from Peking first informed the Western world of acupuncture. The first in depth account of acupuncture in a Western language was written in the 1930's by Soulie de Morant, a French Sinologist and diplomat.

Acupuncture involves the insertion of special needles (usually very thin, and made of gold or silver) into any of about 700 specific points in the body in order to stimulate or to sedate the flow of energy. The type of needle selected, the point selected, the insertion technique, depth of insertion, the angle of insertion and the duration of time that the needle remains inserted are all important aspects of correct acupuncture treatment.

2. **Moxibustion.** This treatment involves the burning of herbs over certain acupuncture points. This produces a deep heat affect on the points. Sometimes the moxi is burnt at the end of an acupuncture needle to produce a combined effect.

3. **Herbs.** This treatment seeks to change the yin and yang distribution via an internal direction, that is, digestion or direct blood absorption. Herbs usually supply something which is deficient in the body in heavier doses than foods generally contain. Taking herbs can be compared to taking drugs or medicine to heal. Herbology is an art that is practiced world-wide. Many of Western medicine's greatest cures are derived from extracts of ancient herbal remedies which have been used for thousands of years. Every country has its unique floral growth and its particular herbal remedies, but modern medical science has yet to explore and test many of these. Anyone interested in herbology should first explore the herbal cures which are indigenous to their own particular location. Herbology teaches that the environment which produces the malady will itself produce the remedy. Thus the yin and the yang will be found close together.

4. **Massage.** An-mo in Chinese, Shiatsu in Japanese and Acupressure in English is the use of the fingers or hand to stimulate the acupuncture points. Although not considered to be as powerful as acupuncture or moxibustion, massage can be very useful for emergency first aid treatment to injuries, for minor problems such as headaches, cramps, backaches, stomach problems and for a general tonification of the body by the

balancing of the yin and yang in the meridians. If acupressure is done regularly it will greatly aid in preventing illness and in maintaining good health.

5. **Exercise.** Both physical and breathing exercises (Chi Kung) have traditionally been acknowledged in Chinese Medicine as effective curative and preventative treatments against disease. Examine the very word "disease"; dis-ease—the "absense of ease". When there is tension (dis-ease) in the body, it is not functioning properly. Muscles, blood vessels, glands and meridians all malfunction, and sickness is the result. Tai Chi Chuan teaches the ancient elixer of life, namely, *relaxation* for better health and longer living.

Physical Exercises. Physical exercises improve muscle tone and stimulate the heart. Muscles and tendons can be stretched for greater flexibility and suppleness. Meridians can also be stretched. This allows for improved circulation of Chi. Dr. George Goodheart[2] discovered that there is a direct relationship between weak muscles and energy imbalance in the meridians related to those muscles. When Tai Chi is performed daily it strengthens the heart, massages the liver, kidneys and internal organs, stretches the meridians and strengthens the muscles related to them.

The different postures in the Tai Chi form are designed to benefit the different organs. For example, the "Single Whip" is designed to help the lungs. "Brush Knee" helps the lower digestive tract and stomach, etc. The Tai Chi form demands that the head, chest and hips (more specifically the nose, solar-plexis and navel) be perfectly aligned. At the same time the practitioner must always be looking at exactly where he is striking or defending. Since the head does not move independently of the torso, it is the eyes which must move left and right, or up and down. Thereby, the eye muscles are exercised and strengthened which promotes better vision. Regular performance of Tai Chi, with deep postures, exercises the connective tissues on the skeletal frame, resulting in greater flexibility and greater blood circulation to the bones. This means greater supplies of oxygen and minerals to the bones and a healthier skeletal frame. A healthier bone marrow will produce a greater supply of red and white corpuscles which will supply the entire body with more oxygen and anti-bodies for better cellular respiration and greater ability for fighting infections.

In the last few years some new discoveries have been made related to the thymus gland. It has been found that the thymus gland is largely responsible for the "immuno-logical surveillance" system in the body. This means that the thymus gland is responsible for ridding the body of foreign germs and infections which, if left unchecked, would cause illness and disease. Lymphocytes (white blood corpuscles) are formed in the bone marrow, they then travel to the thymus gland where they mature and travel to the lymph nodes and spleen. There they give rise to "T cells" (thymus-derived cells). Thymus hormones traveling through the blood system exert influence over the T cells. T cells are directly concerned with resistance to infections and cancer. Actually this idea is not new. As early as 1802 cancer research was done by Dr. Foulerton, an English doctor using thymus extracts to treat cancer. It has subsequently been discovered that stress can cause the thymus gland to send these T cells into the body, thus depleting the gland of its necessary ammunition to fight off an attack against a potential infection. It has also been found that a state of relaxation, contentment and calm will keep the thymus gland operating at its utmost efficiency and allow it to maintain a strong reserve of T cells for combating disease. John Diamond M.D., president of the International Academy of

Preventive Medicine and recipient of the Naughton-Manning Prize for Psychiatry, states: "I have never seen a patient with a chronic degenerative illness who did not have an underactive thymus gland . . . . I believe that it is the thymus weakness, or underactivity, that is the original cause of the illness. All illnesses start with a diminuation of the Life Energy. Should this decrease continue, some organ of the body will be the target for the illness."[3] Dr. Diamond also says the "Life Energy" is what the Chinese call "Chi." Furthermore, he believes that the thymus gland is the organ that regulates the distribution of Chi through the body meridians, from its centralized location within the chest. He points out that the thymus gland can be thought of as the link between the mind and the body, in that, it is the first organ to be affected by stress. Dr. Diamond states six factors which can strongly affect the thymus gland: 1. stress, 2. emotional attitudes, 3. posture, 4. food, 5. social environment, and 6. physical environment. Whenever we practice Tai Chi Chuan at least three of the above six mentioned factors will improve; this in turn will help the thymus gland to operate at its maximum efficiency. It is most important to keep two concepts about health and Tai Chi in the foreground of our minds: 1. The primary and cardinal principle of Tai Chi Chuan is *relaxation*. If one learns nothing else when studying Tai Chi they should at least strive to learn to become more relaxed. With concentration and practice this is accomplished more and more. 2. With increased relaxation we are moving farther and farther away from disease. Stressful mental attitudes which can cause psycho-somatic conditions are dissipated before the disease can take root, and the thymus gland can act more efficiently to ward off foreign bodies such as infections and cancer early while these potential threats have not yet had the time nor the conditions necessary to overrun the body.

Breathing exercises (Chi Kung). Tai Chi Chuan is a form of Chi Kung. Chi Kung (Chi Mastery) is an exercise through which one gains control over the breath energy. When we breathe we take in Chi. Breath control strengthens the Chi-energy of the body. Two important aspects of Chi Kung practice are: relaxation of the entire body and mind, and breathing with attention. It is claimed that one round of Tai Chi Chuan[4] will cause the Chi to circulate one complete round through all the meridians of the entire body. If this claim is true it means that Tai Chi greatly accelerates the circulation of Chi through the meridians, therefore supplying greater health--giving energy to all the organs and glands. This is accomplished when the breath and attention is synchronized with the constantly shifting weight distribution in the Tai Chi form. This unique movement (foreward-backward, open-close) is continuously making parts of the body yin and yang, and is actually pumping Chi through the meridians faster, thus bathing the meridians and cells with health-giving energy. The intense concentration on deep breathing and relaxation leads to a calming of the nervous system which will also strengthen the health. Tai Chi is an internal self-administered massage. Body tone improves and susceptibility to illness decreases. With better health, greater relaxation and deeper breathing, it is said that the aging process will slow down and that the life expectancy will increase. Research in China has convinced the government that the benefits of Tai Chi Chuan are so dynamic that the exercise which was initially discouraged by the communist government has now been formally incorporated into the public schools.

Tai Chi Chuan is the sine qua non—the culmination of thousands of years of tradition, study and knowledge of the body and the composite result of all this wisdom. It is an eclectic blend of the best that Chinese culture and knowledge concerning health has produced.

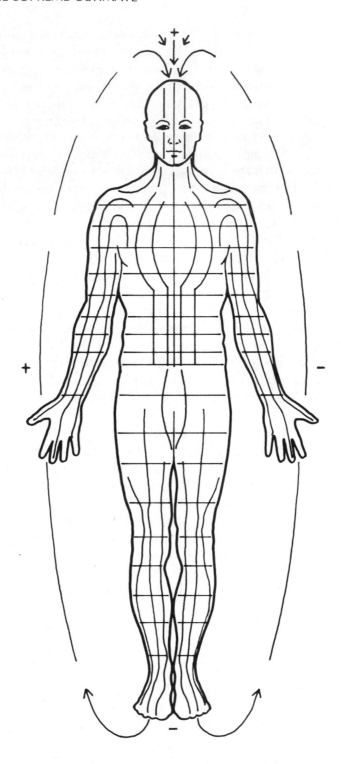

Energy Lines
The constantly shifting weight distribution of the Tai Chi form pumps Chi through the meridians, and promotes the flow of the caduceus energy which enters through the head (the Positive Pole) and exits through the feet (the Negative Pole). The constant turning of the waist (left and right) stimulates the horizontal line of energy.

6. Diet. Correcting the diet can often cure a dysfunction in the system. Conversely, a poor diet or eating something which has adverse effects on one's body, can render other types of treatment virtually ineffective. Our food must provide us with all of the vitamins, minerals, proteins and carbohydrates necessary for proper nourishment. Therefore, knowledge of nutrition is basic to good health. In addition, our food is one of our most important sources of Chi. Everytime we eat we are receiving Chi. Each food has its own yin and yang energy content. Therefore, the diet that we consume is a powerful determinent in our make-up. Certain foods are rich in their supply of Life Energy or Chi, other foods are pathetically drained of Chi. One has only to look at a plate of fresh spinach salad and a plate of canned spinach to dramatize the difference in life energy content. Boiling, overcooking, food processing (called refining or polishing), etc., depletes food of its health-giving life energy. The addition of chemicals—additives, preservatives, food colorings, pesticides—acts as a poison and greatly weakens the body's supply of Chi. In the U.S.A. most meats which are available have been injected with steroids, or other hormones which greatly mutilate and/or destroy the value of the food. In fact, processed foods, sprayed crops, and injected cattle and poultry may be more dangerous than beneficial. Any chemical or additive in excess acts as a poison to the body. Water which is treated with chemicals such as fluoride or chlorine can eventually harm those who drink it. The air we breathe is part of our diet. Air polluted with exhaust fumes, industrial waste, or radiation is poisonous to all who inhale it. Dr. John Gofman, physician and nuclear physicist, and a pioneer in the field of nuclear energy, says that one one millionth of a gram of Plutonium inhaled, will absolutely cause lung cancer. One pound could cause cancer to every man, woman and child on earth.

A nuclear reactor produces between 400 and 500 lbs. of Plutonium annually. It has a half-life of 24,400 years and remains poisonous for over half a million years. Once this substance is produced it is virtually indestructible. It has been estimated that by the year 2000 A.D. over 1.5 million pounds of Plutonium may be produced. Scientists still have not found a safe way of dealing with this deadly nuclear waste problem.[5]

Drugs (which include alcohol, nicotine, and caffeine) if used continuously or recklessly, can also contaminate the body and will act as any other poison in our system. It is certainly no great wonder that the two greatest diseases in the U.S.A. are cancer and heart disease. Cancer is a product of all the poisons that enter and irritate our bodies. One need only look at what the average American consumes daily to see why. Almost all packaged foods bought in supermarkets contain additives, preservatives, sugar and salt. The consumer should develop the habit of reading the ingredients (which are listed in order of concentration) on the labels of each item and familiarizing himself with the effects of the additives before he or she decides to make a purchase.

Students often ask me about diet and foods to be avoided. The following list will be useful to anyone interested in preserving good health.[6]

AVOID:

1. *Additives:* Preservatives, artificial colorings and flavorings, M.S.G.*, etc. These build up in the body to form powerful toxins, causing cancer and other problematic disorders.

---

* Special note to Tai Chi and martial arts students: When you are at your favorite Chinese restaurant, specify "no M.S.G." and watch how much tea you drink (Caffeine).

2. *Bleached flower:* Grains should constitute a large portion of one's diet. Polished flour is stripped of its nutritional value and its life energy as well. Buy only whole grain breads and cakes with no preservatives added.

3. *Polished rice:* Like processed flour, polished rice is nearly void of nutritional content. This should be realized especially in underdeveloped countries where malnutrition is a problem. Eat brown rice.

4. *Refined Sugar (Sucrose):* Nearly all of the sugar available in the U.S.A. is refined sugar. It has no nutritional value. It produces vascular disorders, hypoglycemia and, in large quantities, cancer.

5. *Salt:* Common table salt is 99.5% NaCl—a poison in large doses. In the U.S.A. virtually every food product has this salt added to it. It produces nervousness, anxiety, high blood pressure and heart attacks—the biggest killer in the U.S.A. Use only kelp or Sea Salt, sparingly. Sea Salt contains only 1.5% NaCl and nutrients make up the remaining contents.

6. *Caffeine:* Coffee, tea, and colas contain Caffeine. Caffeine is a stimulant which destroys vitamin B. Any wonder that many children of the "cola-generation" are hyperactive and difficult to manage?

7. *Meats and poultry:* Most meats and poultry are injected with steroids or other hormones, which are believed to be very high contributors to cancer. Meat contains 40% fat and takes an excessively long time to digest. This may irritate the digestive tract and can eventually result in cancer of the colon—the most widespread type of cancer in the U.S.A.

8. *Over eating:* Two meals a day is actually healthier than three. Don't stuff yourself at meals. Ancient Eastern advice is to fill ½ of the stomach with food and ¼ with liquid. The remaining ¼ of the stomach should remain empty.

DO:
• Eat a balanced diet consisting of a variety of whole foods: vegetables, fruits, milk, eggs, grains, legumes, nuts and seeds, (meat, fish, and poultry).*
• Take only natural vitamins extracted from foods—not synthesized from chemicals.
• Chew foods well—this simple act aids in digestion and is reputed to heighten the Chi output of food.

Doctors the world over have long realized the health-giving value of correct diet and often prescribe changes of diet to their patients. The more conscious we become of our health, the less we will contaminate ourselves with poisons and the more we will turn to a healthy diet as a rich source of health-giving Life Energy (Chi). Our health is our only real material wealth! Often, however, the value of health is only realized when it is too late.

Sexuality

According to Taoism, Chi is derived from many sources. It may be obtained from the air that we breathe, from the foods that we eat and from the liquids that we drink.

* Contrary to popular belief, animal protein is not essential. Many vegetables, fruits, grains, nuts and seeds are all excellent sources of *complete* proteins when properly combined.

We can absorb it from the earth when our stance and posture are correct, and we can acquire it from touching another person with a higher energy level. This transmission of energy through touch is the basis of the Taoist teaching on Chi and sexuality. Chi can be passed from one person to another and then circulated back again. As this circulation continues it gains in momentum and in strength, creating an intense energy flow between the two. When the male and female life energies are blended harmoniously together (yin and yang), we have the Tai Chi—the Supreme Ultimate. Taoism teaches that when sexuality is performed "correctly" it is an energizing and life-giving process for both parties. As in all teachings pertaining to Tai Chi, calmness, control and mastery over the self are the keys to higher states of experience. When the sexual act is performed "incorrectly", one or both parties are drained of health-giving Chi. When people operate on a low level of mastery over their bodies, drives and desires, the sexual act can produce anxiety and frustration. An inability (for either sex) to attain an orgasm is seen as a symptom of tension or energy imbalance in the body.

Taoists claimed that the egg and sperm are the sources of life and that Chi is concentrated in them. Sexual energy is Chi, and it is believed that this Chi culminates in orgasm. Since the egg is internal and is not emitted during orgasm, women were encouraged to have orgasms during sexual intercourse. This would enable women to circulate their sexual energies internally and to pass this energy to their male partner. Males do emit sperm during ejaculation, therefore, while they were encouraged to have orgasms, ejaculation was considered a loss of Chi and was reserved only for those times when conception of children was desired. Taoists claimed that males should not dissipate semen for mere sensual pleasure, as this shortens the duration of the sexual union and the joy derived from it. With relaxation and a calm mind, mastery over one's sexual drives is accomplished; then the sexual act can be extended for any desired length of time. Orgasms are experienced, but the quality of these orgasms becomes more refined and takes on a more spiritual significance which bestows a profound state of ecstasy over the entire body and mind. This peace-giving serenity is "bliss". The Taoists encouraged eroticism in order to arouse and heighten sexual energy so that Chi might be cultivated and utilized for greater health, longevity and bliss for both partners. Needless to say, an act of total sexuality is rare, but when attained the two bodies blend into embodiments of Tai Chi (yin and yang) calmly and perfectly united in Tao.

The sexual arts were studied to such a high level in ancient China that the effect of each sexual posture on each organ in the body was documented. Different postures would stretch or massage different meridians and internal organs. It even became common for doctors to prescribe specific sexual postures, specific amounts of times per week, at specific hours of the day, to cure sicknesses.[7]

In India a similar philosophy existed called Tantra Yoga. Tantra Yoga is the path of attaining union with God (Brahman) through the physical union of the opposites—male and female (Shiva and Shakti). Ancient tantric rituals were practiced by priests and priestesses in order to experience the Ultimate. These rituals were depicted in carvings done in temples of worship. A study of these erotic carvings shows that the postures depicted often required abnormal flexibility of the body and therefore a mastery of Hatha (physical) Yoga. The postures would often allow for little or no mobility by the practitioners. This stillness provided a profound meditative state of spiritual serenity where concentration on the union of opposites would be possible. In Indian Tantra, as in Taoist sexual practices, the male was to abstain from ejaculation and to sustain the ecstatic union for as long as desired. Needless to say such intimate depths cannot be attained during casual sexual encounters. Sexuality encompassing spiritual dimension requires conscious and concerted effort by both partners.

Later, the Swiss psychiatrist Dr. Carl Jung, formulated his theory of "anima-animus" which was the Western equivelant of yin and yang and is therefore, in perfect alignment with Taoism and Tantra. Jung called the unconscious feminine part of the males's psyche the anima. The unconscious masculine part of the female's psyche, he termed the animus. He claimed that the attraction of the sexes for one another and their striving for union was actually the seeking for union and wholeness with the unconscious aspects of themselves.[8]

Sex is a healthy and natural physical exercise. Its importance is being recognized in Western medicine more and more. Conversely, the ill effects of poor or unsatisfactory sex lives and the physical and psychological damage caused by indiscriminate sexual encounters is also being realized and examined.

Tai Chi Research

There has been relatively little scientific research done on the effects of Tai Chi Chuan on human physiology. The majority of research has been done in China, but hardly any of this has been translated into English. When discussing research that has been done in China on Tai Chi Chuan, it is also appropriate to mention some research done on Chi Kung—respiratory therapy. This therapy utilizes the same breathing techniques which are basic to Tai Chi Chuan. Both aim to produce more Chi. It follows that if Chi is the health-giving life and energy, an increase of Chi will improve the organic harmony of the body. According to Stephan Palos, author of *The Chinese Art of Healing*, research at the First Medical Academy in Shanghai on Chi Kung respiratory therapy has proven that when employing this breathing, "Exhalation stimulates the parasympathetic part of the nervous system, whereas inhalation does the same for the sympathetic part...ailments due to disorders of the autonomic nervous state can be cured by respiratory exercises."[9] Mr. Palos also states that respiratory therapy is practiced in numerous medical establishments in modern China. The Medical Academies in Shanghai and in Tangshan are partilularly renowned in this field. The chief research in Shanghai is concerned with stomach and intestinal disorders. The Tangshan Academy is chiefly concerned with patients suffering from consumption. The following results are listed:[10]

1958 Statistics for the Shanghai center:

Illness	Number of cases tested	Number completely cured	% of cases positively influenced
Duodenal ulcers	21	13	100%
Duodenal ulcers with prolapse of the stomach	12	4	100%
Prolapse of the stomach	8	5	100%

Cases of stomach and intestinal ailments with special symptoms:[11]

Symptoms	Number of cases	Number completely cured	% positively influenced
Lack of appetite	15	13	100%
Depression	4	4	100%
Nervous breakdown	8	8	100%
Eructation	32	19	100%
Vomiting of gastric acid	27	20	100%
Stomach pains	40	22	100%
Abdomen distension	39	26	100%
Black stool	3	3	100%

Dr. Liu Kui-chen, director of Tangshan sanatorium, published a paper in 1957 entitled *The Practice of Respiratory Therapy (Chi-Kung Liao-fa Shih-chien)*. Dr. Liu reports some 500 successfully treated patients suffering from neurovegetative disorders and diseases of the gastro-intestinal tract, using respiratory therapy alone.[12]

At Shanghai Sanatorium for Respiratory Therapy electrical potential differences on meridians were measured using an "electroencephalograph" and an "acupuncture point micro-ammeter" before and after respiratory therapy. The following data collected from 123 cases of consumption and 49 cases of stomach trouble reveals:

Meridian	index figure before therapy	index figure after 40 minutes of therapy
Lung	47/48	50/52
Large Intestine	42/43	45/46
Heart	37/37	37/38
Small Intestine	44/46	48/49
Spleen	43/45	55/56
Kidney	41/41	45/46
Liver	45/46	49/50
Bladder	40/40	44/46
Gall Bladder	30/31	32/36
Stomach	45/45	51/52

The higher numerical figures indicate a greater electrical potential (greater energy through the meridians). The closer together the numerical figures, the greater the balance indicated within the meridians.[13]

In the 1978-79 edition of Rehabilitation World, Vol. 4, #4, in an article called "Inaccessible China", Edward A. Rust, editor of the journal, describes his visit to The People's Republic of China and a visit to Wushih sanatorium established in 1951. Wushih treats patients with non-infectious chronic diseases such as stroke, heart trouble and rheumatism. Mr. Rust reports, "In the courtyard groups of patients were practicing traditional Chinese 'shadow-boxing' exercises (Tai Chi Chuan), as well as similar exercises using wooden swords'' (Tai Chi Sword form).[14]

In China's mental institutions Tai Chi Chuan is also prescribed as a rehabilitative therapy for the mentally disturbed. It provides the scattered or erratic mental energies of the patient with his own body as a focusing point. This concentration exercise helps the patient's mind. As he increases awareness of his body's tensions and strives to correct them, his body benefits. As his body improves so also do his mental faculties. When his body and mind are relaxed and unified he is in greater control over himself once again.

Research in the U.S.A.

Tai Chi Chuan Project #1

In 1975, I was working as an analytical chemist for the Chief Medical Examiners Office, located at the Bellevue-N.Y.U. Medical Complex in New York City. Because I was aware of the use of Tai Chi in China as a therapy for the mentally disturbed, I decided that this would be an excellent opportunity to test this exercise with mental patients in a New York City hospital. First I obtained Master Cheng's permission, then I volunteered to set up an experimental program at Bellevue Psychiatric Hospital. The project lasted four months. Unfortunately, the experiment had to be cut short because of the N.Y.C. lay-offs which dismissed many of the project's personnel. Therefore, long range experimental data could not be properly collected. Nevertheless, it was a very revealing experiment for me and for those people who were directly involved with the project. Many referred to it as the most successful theraputic program ever set up at Bellevue. The patients enjoyed it and subjectively reported that they felt greatly benefited by doing the exercises. Often I worked individually with patients and assigned specific postures to be practiced. I noted that certain moves were particularly enjoyable and easy for the patients, such as ''The Opening'', and that other moves were difficult. I also noted that it was usually not wise to teach these patients the entire form, because the long and exact sequence of moves would be too tedious. So rather than frustrate the patients with such long sequences and such difficult moves, I found that modifying, editing or just assigning specific postures to practice worked better for them.

The following report was written by Dr. John Beaulieu, on his assessment of the project. Dr. Beaulieu worked closely with me at the time of the project and I am grateful to him for his enthusiasm in promoting the experiment.

THE TAI CHI CHUAN PROJECT
BELLEVUE PSYCHIATRIC HOSPITAL, N.Y.C.
FEBRUARY 1975 - MAY 1975

Introduction:

The idea for the Tai Chi Chuan Project first began in the Activity Therapy Director's office of Bellevue Psychitric Hospital. Mr. Lawrence Galante submitted a proposal for the introduction of Tai Chi Chuan to our patients. As Activity Therapy Superviser, I had been chosen to determine the feasibility of the project at Bellevue. Several discussion followed concerning the nature of Tai Chi, the various ways in which it could be presented, its benefits, and possible applications in our hospital setting.

What impressed me most about the meetings was the flexibility and adaptability of the "Tai Chi system". That is, without sacrificing or compromising any of the basic Tai Chi principles—yielding, centering, relaxation, balance, etc.—we were able to create a structure for the introduction of Tai Chi Chuan at Bellevue Psychiatric Hospital which did not interfere with or disrupt normal hospital procedure in any way.

Overall Project Goals:
1. To provide an opportunity for *staff and patients* to learn together. Being basically non-verbal, Tai Chi tends to be non-threatening and therefore, provides an excellent medium for both staff and patients to meet on a safe level which transcends normal hospital roles.
2. To allow each participant an opportunity to develop a "new body awareness" which emphasizes relaxation rather than tension. Clients in psychiatric hospitals have and are undergoing high levels of stress. This stress is reflected in body holding patterns, such as raised shoulders, stiff knee joints, rigid facial expressions, etc. Tai Chi, with its emphasis on relaxation through body awareness, provides an excellent non-threatening milieu for clients to relearn a basic trust in their bodies. This trust is reflected in an increased ability to tolerate higher levels of stress without having to activate emotional and physical armoring systems.
3. To allow each participant an opportunity to experience the practical application of Tai Chi principles in every day life. To always be relaxed, balanced, and centered in our current technological society is a long-range goal, however, it is a goal worthy of attainment. Through Tai Chi our clients were provided with a practical internal experience and given specific information as to how that experience could improve the quality of their lives. The ability to remain relaxed, balanced and centered in the face of everyday stress is a challenge which is not met by brute force but by gentle, aware yielding. As the client's ability to experience the relaxed centered state grew, so did their awareness of themselves when they were not in that state. Experiences like this provided excellent material for verbal discussion groups on handling stress.

Implementation Structure:
Two programs were initiated: 1. A "noon hour" Tai Chi group for staff and patients which met from 12:30-1:00 once a week in the 7th. floor leisure room.
2. A client-centered Tai Chi group for out-patients which met once a week in the out-patient clinic under the guidance of the Socializing Group Program.

Both programs were led by Mr. Lawrence Galante. The first emphasized the traditional Tai Chi form and principles, the second emphasized individual Tai Chi movements and immediate practical experience of the Tai Chi principles.

Initial Evaluation:
Group 1 (noon hour) attracted 35 persons—10 Activity Therapists, 6 Social Workers, 3 Nurses, 2 Psychologists, 2 Psychiatrists, 4 Nurses Aids, and 8 out-patients. Due to erratic schedules of hospital staff and clients the attendance at this group varied radically over the course of the project, however verbal support from all staff members participating (whether in attendance or not) continued for the duration of the project. I personally can say that it was one of the few hospital programs during which I experienced no hostility and a tremendous amount of support.

Group 2. The patient group maintained a steady attendance and appeared (no formal measurement was taken) to maintain a high interest level in their discussion on what they were learning and its practical application in their daily lives. Several patients, (after a time lapse of 4 years) still practice the movements and principles that they learned in the original Tai Chi group.

Conclusion:

Due to the N.Y.C. budget cuts and layoffs, the project was terminated in May of 1975 making a complete objective evaluation impossible. However, in my subjective opinion, the project was successful and I would, if circumstances permitted, re-implement Tai Chi at Bellevue.

Tai Chi is a natural and safe vehicle for both clients and staff to learn and experience the benefits of being able to channel, concentrate and co-ordinate their bodies and minds; to learn to relax and to "neutralize" rather than resist the stress in their personal lives. This is an ability which we greatly need to nurture in our modern fast-paced society.

Dr. John Beaulieu N.D., M.T.R.S.
Supervisor of Activity Therapy
Bellevue Psychiatric Hospital N.Y.C.
Currently Assistant Professor of
Theraputics Recreation at C.U.N.Y.

Tai Chi Chuan Project #2

In 1978 my colleague, Leonard Antonucci,and I decided to avail ourselves of the combined resources at our disposal, and to conduct some scientific investigations into Tai Chi Chuan. Both Mr. Antonucci and myself are scientists; he was formally associated with the Applied Physiology Laboratory of the Health Science Dept. at Long Island University, and holds a Masters degree in Physiology. We were advanced students under Grand Master Cheng Man-ch'ing and both taught Tai Chi Chuan and other styles of oriental martial arts for many years.

We decided to observe and evaluate the effects of Tai Chi Chuan on the cardio-vascular system and to try to determine if Tai Chi is a valid form of exercise for stimulating cardio-vascular development.

Our basis for making a determination was the criteria set down by the American Heart Association. The A.H.A. has determined that an exercise is valid for cardio-vascular development if it can stimulate the heart to beat at a rate of between 60-80% of the maximum heart rate and maintain that rate for a minimum of twenty minutes per day, three times per week.[15] The A.H.A. has stated that exercise producing amounts greater than 85% of maximum heart rate (M.H.R.) can be harmful and dangerous because it places too great a strain on the heart. On the other hand, exercise producing less than 60% M.H.R. does not stimulate the heart enough for proper cardiac development.

The heart beating at 60-80% M.H.R. is like an automobile with an optimal cruising range of 40-50 mp.h.. Within this range it is most efficient and there is less wear and tear on the engine. At speeds lower or greater, it is less efficient and the potential of engine breakdown increases.

Experiment

Is Tai Chi Chuan a valid form of exercise to stimulate cardio-vascular development? The following experiment was conducted at the Applied Physiology Laboratory at Long Island University, in Brooklyn, N.Y., in 1978.

Terms and Definitions:
1. Electro- Cardiogram (E.K.G., or E.C.G.): An electrical instrument that records the electrical impulses of heart activity.
2. Cardiac Cycle: Electrical wave form produced by an E.K.G. during one complete atrial and ventricular systole (heart contraction).
3. Heart Rate: The number of cardiac cycles per minute as recorded by an Electro-Cardiogram.
4. Maximum Heart Rate (M.H.R.): The maximum number of complete contractions that the heart can accomplish in one minute.

M.H.R. is dependent upon age, not physical conditioning. Two workers of the same age will both have the same M.H.R., but the one in superior physical condition can do more work, and endure more strain, before his M.H.R. is reached. A general formula for determing M.H.R. is 220 minus one's age (M.H.R. = 220-age).

Method:
Twenty–five students (ages 20-60), were selected who had been practicing Tai Chi Chuan for a period of from 1-7 years.

Heart rate was measured by a Telematry Electro-Cardiogram which consisted of two electrodes placed on the subject's chest, (on the Manubrium and on the V5 positions) which fed into a miniature portable transmitter (weighing ½ lb.) strapped to the subject's waist. An electrical signal of the subject's heart activity was then transmitted to a receiver which fed into an E.K.G. recorder, producing a wave graph of the electrical activity occuring in the subject's heart.[16] A pre-exercise heart rate was taken with the subject in a standing position. The subject was next instructed to perform the Tai Chi form in the "high" position (knees only slightly bent). A ten second E.K.G. was taken at the end of every minute. Another E.K.G. reading was taken at the conclusion of the Tai Chi form and again after one and two minutes of rest. The twenty–five subjects then returned the following week and the above procedure was repeated in the "low" position (knees bent as much as possible, stances as long and low as possible). The form lasts approximately 7-9 minutes (Yang style short form). The chart below summarizes the data.

Findings:
Some sources state that Tai Chi is effortless for the heart, others say that it increases heart strength. Our experiment showed that either may occur, depending upon whether the Tai Chi form is done with the knees relatively unbent (high position) or if it is done with the knees very bent (low position).

We found that the height of the form performance was the factor which determined the difference in heart rate. When the Tai Chi is performed in the low position, great cardio-vascular (heart) stimulation occurs (between 60-80% of M.H.R.). When the Tai Chi form is performed in a high position there is very little heart stimulation produced (less than 60%).

Often it is necessary for people recuperating from heart attacks or from heart surgery to stimulate and strengthen the heart. Conventional exercises, however, tend to produce too much exertion and stress on the heart. Doing a "high" Tai Chi form, therefore, could be ideal as it may produce a heart rate of about 20% above normal.

This is a hypothesis which we feel should be explored by cardiologists and other cardiovascular experts. Several students of mine with medical histories of heart disease have reported that after doing Tai Chi their doctors have informed them of a marked improvement in their condition. The students also expressed marked feelings of improved health and general well-being.

Summarization of data on Project #2:

#	Subject	Age	Max	Target H.R.	H.F.	L.F.
1-	S.L.	21	199	119-159	98	166
2-	S.S.	21	199	119-159	112	136
3-	A.A.	21	199	119-159	92	132
4-	L.F.	25	195	117-156	104	148
5-	S.G.	25	195	117-156	98	148
6-	C.C.	28	192	115-153	98	136
7-	H.P.	28	192	115-153	120	136
8-	K.P.	28	192	115-153	92	126
9-	J.W.	28	192	115-153	108	116
10-	J.R.	29	191	114-152	98	148
11-	V.A.	29	191	114-152	86	137
12-	P.B.	30	190	114-152	88	124
13-	F.O.	31	189	113-151	100	132
14-	L.A.	32	188	112-150	92	154
15-	D.G.	32	188	112-149	92	120
16-	M.B.	33	187	112-149	104	124
17-	S.N.	33	187	112-149	76	114
18-	G.F.	34	186	111-149	104	132
19-	L.G.	36	184	110-147	104	136
20-	T.D.	36	184	110-147	120	132
21-	J.C.	36	184	110-147	88	122
22-	C.B.	37	183	110-147	106	142
23-	J.H.	38	182	109-145	100	128
24-	D.K.	45	175	105-140	80	112
25-	R.D.	53	167	100-133	116	124

Key
Max.: Maximum age predicted heart rate (220 - age).
Target H.R.: Heart rate that must be achieved during exercise to stimulate cardiovascular improvement as established by the A.H.A. (60%-80% of M.H.R.).
H.F.: Heart rate achieved when the form was done in the "High" position.
L.F.: Heart rate achieved when the form was done in the "Low" position.
Comments:
The average form lasted 7½ minutes.

As can be seen from the chart only two subjects were able to increase their heart rate to the desired level when doing the form in the "High" position, whereas all the subjects were able to do so when doing the form in the "Low" position.

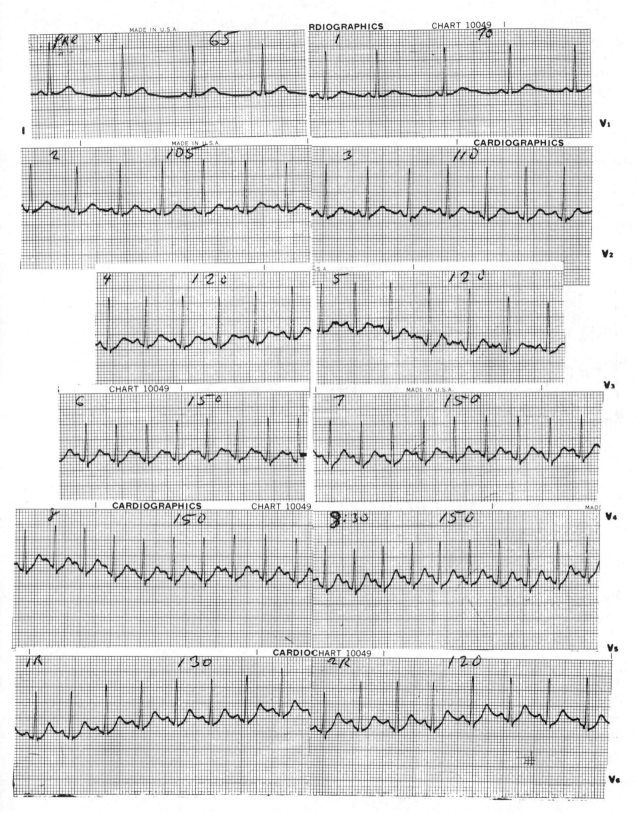

Electro-cardiograph of subject doing the Tai Chi form in the ''low'' position.

The American Heart Association recommends that exercise in the "Target H.R." level be sustained for twenty minutes per day (not necessarily at one stretch without resting) at least three times per week. This can be achieved by doing the Tai Chi form (short version) three times per day. Daily practice is better for the heart than doing exercise only three times per week.

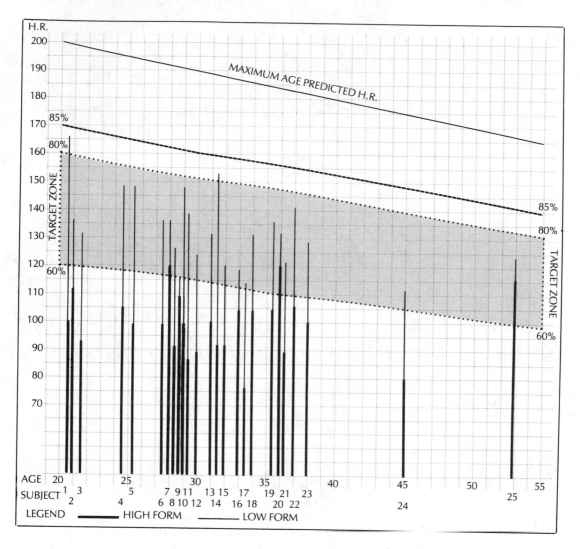

The research projects that I have mentioned represent only a beginning. It is important for reputable Tai Chi teachers, scientists, physiologists and medical doctors to pool their time and talents and explore the effects of Tai Chi Chuan. Through such work our scientific knowledge will grow and an important and accessible manner of healing may be opened up for many.

Tai Chi Chuan and Self-defense

The three main Tai Chi principles which, according to the *Classics*, must be internalized for self-defense purposes are:

1. Correct Concentration
2. Relaxation
3. Chi Development

Tai Chi Chuan is a very conceptual martial art; it relies heavily upon correct concentration. The *Classics* say:

> The mind should come first, the body later.
>
> The body should follow the mind as a shadow follows an object.
>
> All movements are directed by the mind, not by exerting muscular strength.

As I have mentioned throughout this text, relaxation is the cardinal rule of Tai Chi Chuan. The *Classics* tell us: *Give up and follow the opponent*. To give up means to relax completely. Relaxation is a state which requires great mental poise. Next it is necessary to pattern the body after the relaxed state of the mind. This means no tension. Lack of tension creates the correct body poise necessary for utilizing Tai Chi for self-defense. In picturesque language the *Classics* describe the correct poise of the Tai Chi boxer.

> Be alert as a hawk ready to seize a rabbit.
>
> When quiet, resemble a mountain.
>
> When moving, be as a river.
>
> When storing energy, be as a bow with its string drawn.
>
> When releasing energy, be as an arrow being shot.

This ability hinges upon the practitioner's ability to concentrate correctly and to relax completely. The idea of following an opponent is further clarified:

> If the opponent does not move, remain still.
>
> When he is about to move, follow his
> intention and move before him.

With correct relaxation comes the ability to "sink" or to drop one's center. "Sinking" enables us to form a firm foundation, called "rooting". The "root" should be as low as possible. The *Classics* say that correct boxing is:

> Rooted at the feet, extends through the legs,
> is directed by the waist, and is manifested
> through the fingers.
>
> There must be a coordination and unison between
> the feet, legs, waist and fingers.

Developing Chi

The classic goal of the Tai Chi practitioner is the development of Chi. This Chi is an invaluable aid in self-defense. There are many legendary stories of remarkable and seemingly super-human abilities displayed by Tai Chi masters due to their great Chi development.[1] The *Classics* say:

> If Chi is developed no injuries will occur.
>
> Use willpower to move the Chi.

Master Cheng Man-ch'ing would often tell us that unless the student interposes the concept of Chi moving his body, Chi would not be developed. The mind must move the Chi and the Chi must move the body.

$$\text{MIND} \longrightarrow \text{CHI} \longrightarrow \text{BODY.}$$

The Tai Chi literature tells us that unless the breath is consciously coordinated with the movements of a relaxed body and mind, Chi will not be developed. When you breathe, imagine the breath as Chi-energy entering your body. This Chi can perhaps better be visualized as "light". Next imagine this Chi filling all of the body, sinking to the Tan Tien, being stored in the bones, and being extended out through the fingers with every exhalation.

> Let the Chi permeate into the bones.

The Chi must be visualized as centered in the Tan Tien. The Tan Tien holds your vital supply of Chi, which is dispatched upon your conscious command.

> Chi is as refined steel, what strength
> can even compare with it?

When the student of Tai Chi Chuan utilizes the above three principles he is more than just a formidable adversary. When these principles are used in conjunction with the eight major exercises of Tai Chi Chuan his art is on the "heavenly" level.*

Self-Defense?

Often I am asked questions regarding Tai Chi Chuan as a fighting art: Is it really possible to use Tai Chi Chuan for self-defense? Why is it practiced so slowly? Are you supposed to fight using the moves learned in the form in that same particular sequence? How does one know which techniques to use when? How long does it take before Tai Chi can be used for self-defense?

These are a few of the questions that I will attempt to answer. Yes, Tai Chi Chuan really is an ancient form of self-defense originated by masters of Shao-lin Chuan. These monks were creative and gifted enough in their comprehension of the philosophy of Taoism with its principles of yin and yang, to combine their knowledge of Kung Fu and Taoism to invent a more subtle martial art form. Since this new martial art successfully held its own against older, more classic fighting systems it became accepted as a serious and valid system of self-defense in China.

Why so slowly? One only practices slowly to perfect technique, coordination, balance and centering. In an actual fight, one's speed would exactly match the speed of his opponent's attacks. This can only be done if one is relaxed and can move with the attacking force.

No, you do not fight using the moves in the same order as the form. One draws upon the appropriate techniques desired from the form, and uses them. The form contains a basic vocabulary of techniques. A child learns the alphabet from A-Z. He does not use the alphabet in that order. Later he learns to pull from his memory the letters that he will need to form appropriate words.

How does one know which techniques to use? One knows which techniques to use by learning the applications of all of the techniques, visualizing them during practice and later, by practicing these applications with a partner. When fighting one will neither have time to think of which techniques to use nor to calculate proper execution. One can only react. The body reacts in the way it has been trained. A boxer will box, a wrestler will wrestle, a karateka will use Karate, a Shao-lin practitioner will react with Shao-lin, and one trained in Tai Chi Chuan will use Tai Chi Chuan. Also remember that your performance against an opponent will, most probably, be vastly inferior to your solo performance. Therefore, practice seriously and correctly.

How long will it take? This depends on so many factors that the answer varies from one person to another. Before answering I would ask several questions: How much will you practice? How co-ordinated are you? How relaxed are you? What is your capacity to learn to relax? How athletic are you? How alert are you? How well can you concentrate? The opponent's level of "Kung Fu" is another factor that must be carefully taken into account. Certainly there is a great difference between defending yourself against an uncoordinated drunk or against a black belt in Karate. The more skill, training and

*Master Cheng distinguished between three levels of Tai Chi development: 1. Man, 2. Earth, 3. Heaven—the highest.

strength that your opponent has, the more difficult is the task of out-maneuvering, neutralizing and overcoming him. All of these variables, and more, are factors which will determine your rate of progress and your ability to utilize Tai Chi Chuan for self-defense. If I had to give a general answer to the above question, I would say that the person of average ability with no previous martial training should estimate about five to ten years before Tai Chi Chuan is practical against an aggressive attack. Variations are possible however; several students who have studied for only about one year have told me of incidents where they have successfully used Tai Chi for self-defense to avoid cars, bicycles, grabby wise guys on the streets, etc.

The classical sequence of study for the serious student of Tai Chi Chuan is designed to prepare the student for conscious and deliberate ability to defend himself even against a skillfully executed attack. The classical sequence of study for the serious student of Tai Chi Chuan is:

1. The Solo Form.
2. Learning the applications of the postures.
3. Push Hands (first stationary or fixed step).
4. Walking Push Hands.
5. Ta Lu.
6. Weapons Forms.
7. The Two Person Form.
8. Free Hands.

1. **The Solo Form:** One begins studying Tai Chi Chuan by learning the solo Tai Chi form. This form, when done correctly, contains and illustrates all of the essential principles of correct body movement and self-defense. The body must relax completely and perform all the postures correctly.

2. **Learn the applications of the postures.** Each and every posture of the form has several application possibilities. As pictured in the Tai Chi symbol, all aspects of the Tai Chi form are both yin—defensive and yang—aggressive. For example "Play Guitar" is a classic defensive posture, yet when used to break an opponent's arm, it is aggressive. The serious student should make it an assignment to realize what each yin and yang application is for all of the postures. One should visualize an opponent as he goes through the postures. This will give the postures meaning, add to his comprehension, and give solidity to his form.

3. **Push Hands (T'ui Shou):** Traditionally, once the student has learned and corrected the solo form, he begins studying Push Hands. In the first stage one practices Push Hands using only one arm at a time. Next one learns the classical moves of the two-arm Push Hands exercise. Push Hands is an exercise done by two people, using the Ward-off, Rollback, Push, and Press postures in pre-arranged sequence. Again we can say that the objective of this exercise is twofold, yin and yang. It is yin when one is trying to evade all pushes (called "neutralizing") without stepping back or resisting. The *Classics* say:

> With four ounces of strength you can
> deflect one thousand pounds of force.

It is yang when without using brute strength, one tries to uproot an opponent causing both of his feet to leave the ground. This is done by touching the opponent lightly (using the hands like antenna), to perceive his center of gravity. When this center is located one relaxes the arms and upper body completely and shifts his weight towards the opponent, using the movement of the legs and waist for momentum. (See photograph of the "Push Hands" form.)

Basic Principles are:

A) Do not double weight. It is essential that one clearly distinguishes between the yin and yang, full and empty portions of the body. This relates directly to the ability to neutralize and return the attacking force. The *Classics* say:

> Clearly differentiate between the substantial
> and insubstantial parts of the body.

When one does not distinguish between yin and yang it leads to double weighting and consequent loss of balance. This occurs when weight is equally yang (heavy, strong) on two sides of the body.

Examples of Double Weighting:
• when weight is equally distributed (50%) on both legs. This makes maneuvering difficult. When retreating to neutralize, don't turn your waist before shifting to your back leg as this will necessitate your moving into a 50%—50% stance when you shift your weight back.
• when weight is on your right leg and you are pushing with your right hand. This creates a weakness on your left side, and vice versa.
• pushing with two arms at the same time. This weakens the lower part of the body, your stances and foundation. Attack with one hand at a time. Although you may be touching your opponent with two hands, push with only one. The *Classics* say:

> Attack only one point of your opponent.

B) Do not Over-extend. Once the center of gravity is over the front foot you are over-extending. This also affects your balance adversely. You are over-extending when:
• You are in a forward stance and your knee goes beyond your front toe.
• You are leaning forward so that your chest is beyond your front toe.

Remember, in Tai Chi, as in life, when you over-extend you are setting yourself up for a fall! This rule should be strictly observed in all facets of Tai Chi practice.

C) Do not allow your arms to touch your body. This will allow your opponent to get very close to your center. The closer he comes to your center, the easier it will be for him to push you. Maintain Ward-off and Rollback positions to keep him away from your center.

D) When neutralizing, move with your opponent. When defending move at the same speed as your opponent's push. If you move faster than he, you will break contact. This contact is always to the benefit of the defender. While maintaining contact you can control the attacker's hands. If contact is broken it will give your opponent a clearing and he could attempt to push or punch you. Therefore, relax and allow the opponent's push to set your speed of retreat. Withdrawing slower than the push creates a target for your opponent to push against.

E) Do not shift your weight 100% back to avoid his first push. If you do, you will have no room to avoid his press or second attack.

F) Stick to your opponent. Stick to the opponent as though attached, yet be so light that the opponent cannot perceive the touch or intention.

G) Always realize that every push is a potential punch and that many people can deliver devastating and incapacitating blows with their hands. Therefore strive never to allow a push to find a solid surface to push against.

The Solo Form and the Push Hands exercise compliment one another respectively as yin and yang. The Solo Form is yin—passive; Push Hands is yang—aggressive and competitive. Whenever one is pushed during Push Hands, it means that there was a point of resistance or tension which the opponent was able to perceive and push against. The student should immediately do two things:

1. try to eliminate that tension.

2. refer back to the Solo Form—is that corresponding move being practiced incorrectly or with tension? The chances are that the answer is yes. Isolate that move, relax into the posture, and eliminate the tension.

Fixed Push Hands means that the defender is never permitted to step back to evade the attacker; although the attacker is permitted to step forward whenever his opponent is beyond his reach. This rule makes neutralizing the attacker's energy most difficult, but remember, if you can learn to do this, you will have mastered one of the pinnacles of martial art maneuvers, "never resist, yet never be moved".

Master Cheng Man-ch'ing greatly stressed the importance of the stationary Push Hands exercise, because it forces one to stand his ground and really neutralize an attack. This is difficult, but it is excellent practice because situations may occur when you cannot step back or to the side (i.e. when one is surrounded by enemies, or when one is up against a wall) and you will have to neutralize *in place*.

4. **Walking Pushing Hands.** A variation of Push Hands involves both partners stepping together as they practice their arm maneuvers. As player A steps forward with his right foot, player B steps back with his left foot and vice versa. This ability to step, matching precisely your opponent's steps, should be practiced until you have the timing as perfectly as two people doing a fox-trot (dance). This ability to step with an opponent will enable one to evade a charge, side-step, or even to sweep the attacker. In a real fighting situation the option to step back from an attack is usually there and should be used. The student proficient in both Push Hands techniques will have the option of stepping back with the attack and neutralizing, or of standing and neutralizing.

5. **Ta Lu (Great Pulling).** Once Push Hands is learned, one next turns to the Ta Lu exercise. The Ta Lu exercises are a set (usually three—but this may vary depending on the style of Tai Chi Chuan) of choreographed moves done by two people which consist of eight postures: Ward-off, Rollback, Press, Push, Pull, Split, Elbow, and Shoulder. The eight postures correspond to the Pa Kua, eight directions or eight trigrams of the *I Ching*. These postures are combined with multidirectional stepping, attacks, neutralizations, and counter-attacks.

• *Free Style Ta Lu.* When all the Ta Lu exercises are learned the student next tries to spontaneously combine moves together from all of the Ta Lu sets, slowly building up speed without sacrificing precision.

6. **Weapon Forms.** The study of Chinese weapons has always been an integral part of Kung Fu training. Weapon study teaches the student how to extend his energy to any object he is holding in his hand, whether this is a sword, a pen or a shovel. The principle

behind using any weapon is the same and it is always in conformity with the principles of the solo forms in that particular style. Thus in Tai Chi Weapons, the guiding principles are relaxation, coordination, and unity of movement, being centered and extending Chi. The classical weapons used in Tai Chi are the Sword, Staff and Big Knife (Single Edged Sword). Each weapon relates to one of the five elements and each of these weapons will teach the practitioner some unique facet of extending his Chi. When the entire series is learned he is a well-rounded martial artist, ideally capable of utilizing any object in his grasp as an extention of himself and of his Chi.

7. **Two Person Form (San-shou).** The Two Person Form consists of a choreographed series of fighting movements for two people which utilizes the moves of the Solo Form, the Push Hands, the Ta Lu, the Five Elements Posture, Advance, Retreat, Look Left, Gaze Right, and Central Equilibrium and more. It is the logical extension of all of these. This fighting routine is practiced over and over again, learning each attack and neutralization until it can be achieved with expert precision and speed. The Two Person Form is invaluable for learning form application and self-defense.[2]

8. **Free Hands.** When the student is proficient in all of the above exercises he starts creating ad-lib Push Hands situations to simulate sparring and real fighting situations. The aim should be to try and defend against any attack encountered without sacrificing the basic Tai Chi principles. Continuous practice in this and in all of the above exercises will prepare the student for self-defense and combat against any other style of martial art. These exercises should be done faster and faster until real life fighting speed is attained. By using a combination of punches and animal hand maneuvers i.e. Tiger, Crane, Snake, etc., greater variety and flexability of fighting is learned.

Remember that Tai Chi cannot be limited to form practice, nor to self-defense, nor to any other specific situation. Tai Chi is a quality of life and an art of living. When you incorporate Tai Chi into everything you do you will be better able to cope with the vicissitudes of life much more harmoniously and creatively, with less tension and stress. When all of the above principles are comprehended and applied in all aspects of life, then one is truly practicing Tai Chi Chuan!

The Dynamics of
Tai Chi Chuan

The dynamics of Tai Chi Chuan can be illustrated as follows:

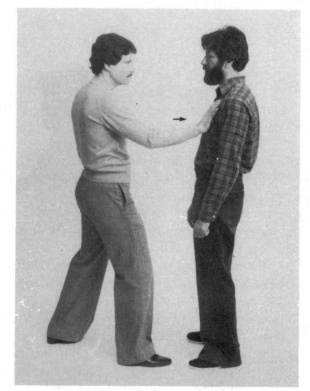

1. B pushes A

Yielding

Returning Energy

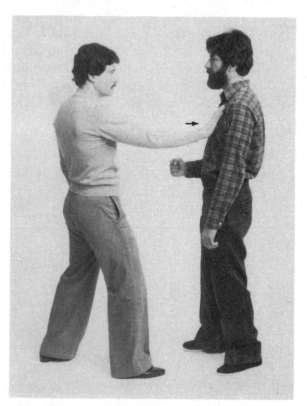

Thus the Tai Chi practitioner conducts the opponent's energy and returns it back to the attacker.

4. B pushes A. A's fist is poised and ready to counterattack.

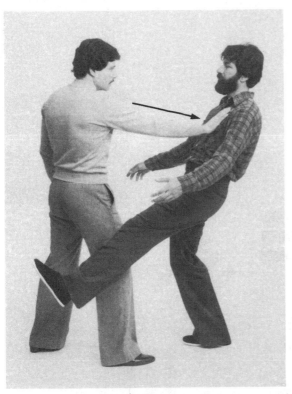

2. If A is rigid (unyielding), he will be pushed.

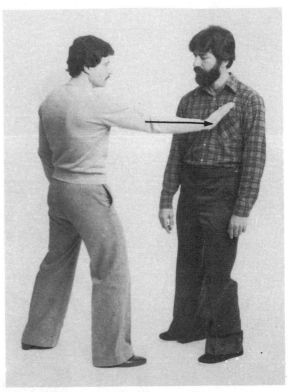

3. If A yields and turns with the attacking force, he will not be pushed. This is called "neutralizing."

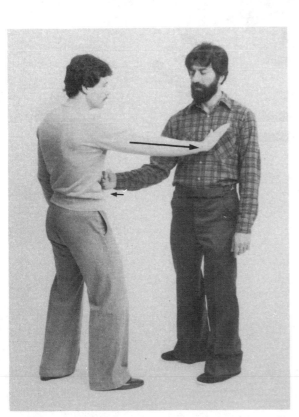

5. When A's left side yields and neutralizes, his right shoulder moves forward.

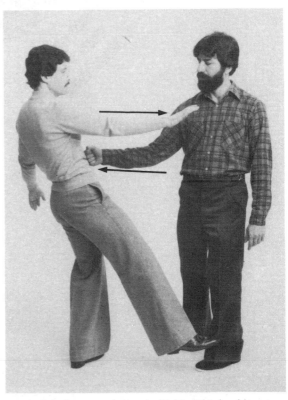

6. A's right fist moves forward with his right shoulder, punching B.

The Solo Form

The Solo Form presented in this book is the "short" Yang style as taught to me by Grand Master Cheng Man-ch'ing. There are, to my knowledge, only two departures from Master Cheng's teachings:

1. He taught the "Parry" (#43 and #177) dropping the right arm near the right leg, instead of bringing it to the waist.

2. The "Repulse Monkey" (#69 to #75) was taught with the feet moving back parallel to each other, rather than at 45° angles.

The changes that I have made are closer to the original form as taught by Grand Master Yang Cheng-fu, my teacher's master. Master Yang's manner of performing these moves is more practical for martial arts application. When I once questioned Master Cheng about the "Parry", he admitted that the way he was teaching it was impractical for fighting, as the arm could not actually be dropped so low. But he told me he was teaching it in this way to promote greater relaxation in the students. Master Cheng was not especially concerned with the martial applications of this art (especially in his later years), rather, he was more concerned with the health and relaxation aspects. One may ask if alterations are legitimate to make. It is a fact that Tai Chi masters have been altering the form from its very beginning. Master Cheng made great Tai Chi modifications from his teacher's form and created the form presented here. Nearly every great Tai Chi master made alterations long before him. The student of Tai Chi must make it his business to duplicate his teacher's form as exactly as possible. Only after you have mastered the moves as your teacher has taught them, and understand them thoroughly, should you even begin to consider changing anything, and that should be done only after extensive research into other possibilites.

With so many variations in the form how is a beginner to ascertain what is correct? Look to the Tai Chi Classics! People may change the outward moves slightly but only if the classical principles are being violated can it be considered wrong. Master Cheng made several movies of himself doing the form in different periods of his life. There are obvious differences in the outer structure of his form when he was younger and when he was older. Yet the Classical principles were adhered to in both of these versions. When selecting a Tai Chi Chuan teacher be certain that he or she knows and adheres to the Classical principles.

Another thing to consider when selecting a Tai Chi instructor, is whether the teacher knows how to use Tai Chi Chuan for self-defense and can give a reasonable demonstration of the art. Master Cheng said that if one cannot utilize these principles on a practical, demonstrable level, then he is not very advanced and should not be teaching Tai Chi Chuan.

The serious Tai Chi student should commit himself to practice the form two times a day (minimum), once in the morning and once in the evening. It is not good to do Tai Chi or any other exercise on a full stomach. One should wait at least one hour after eating before exercising. When one commits oneself to this discipline he will be taking great strides towards a relaxed state of being and good health.

Key

A = Author
B = Attacker
Wt. = Weight
Rt. = right
L = left

When stepping forward, always step with the heel first.
When stepping backward, always step with the toe first.
When you "Step into a forward stance," be certain to step wide, a "shoulder's distance apart." A common error is stepping into a narrow forward stance.

A solid line shows the right hand movement. A broken line shows the left hand movement.

Always keep the elbows and knees slightly bent. NEVER lock them.

"Form a ball with the hands" means to align the palms with one another. This allows energy to pass from one palm to another (positive and negative poles in the hands).

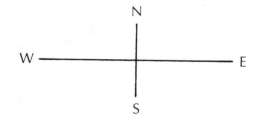

Relative directions are given in the diagrams. When the figure in the photograph is facing the reader he is said to be facing South. This does not mean that the form must actually be performed facing South.

Shoulder's Width

Weight Key

NO WEIGHT

Suspended

0%

Only toe on ground

Only heel on ground

50%

30%

70%

100%

The Tai Chi Form
With Applications of the Major Postures
Section I

1. PREPARATION

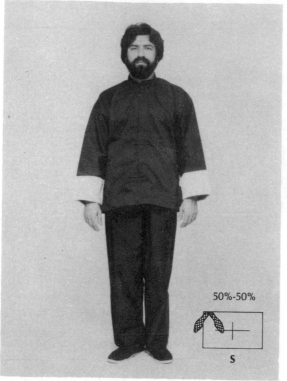

50%-50%

S

Opening posture.

2. OPENING

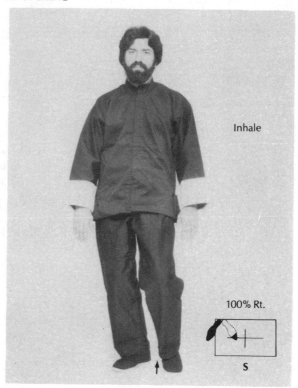

Inhale

100% Rt.

S

Empty and lift L. leg.

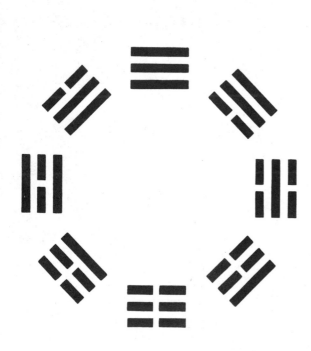

2A. A is balanced on his Rt. leg, leaving his L. leg empty and ready to move, stomp or kick.

3. OPENING

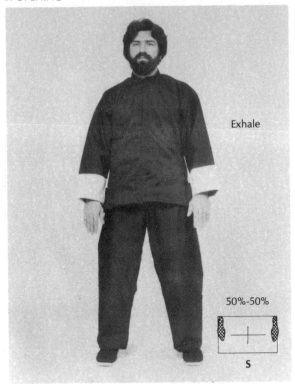

Exhale

50%-50%

S

Place L. toe shoulders' distance to the L. Pivot on L. toe and push L. heel out until foot is straight. Shift weight L. and turn Rt. toe to the L. until both feet are parallel.

4. OPENING

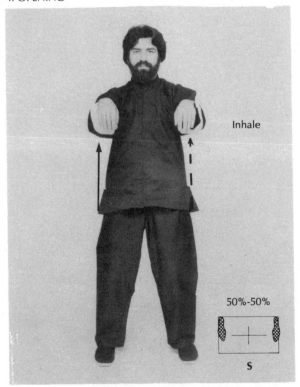

Inhale

50%-50%

S

Raise both wrists to shoulders' height, arms about ¾ extended.

4A. A's rising wrists are used to intercept punches delivered to the mid-section or to strike an opponent.

5. OPENING

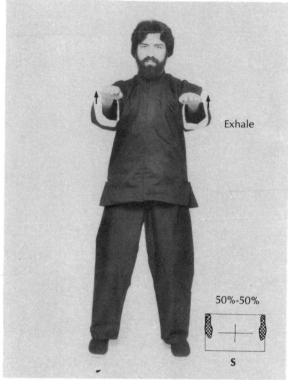

Exhale

50%-50%

S

Straighten wrists, palms face downward; extend fingers.

6. OPENING

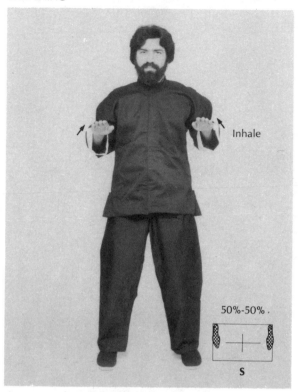

Inhale

50%-50%

S

Withdraw arms towards the chest.

5A. A's straightening wrist and extending fingers are used to counterattack an opponent's eyes or body.

6A. A withdraws his arm and attacks B with his elbows.

8.

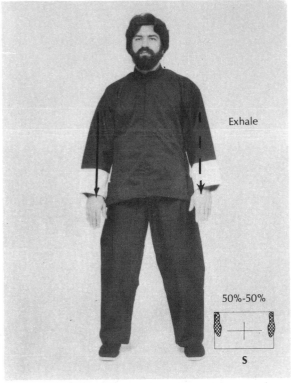

Exhale

50%-50%

S

Lower the arms until they are at your sides, palms facing back.

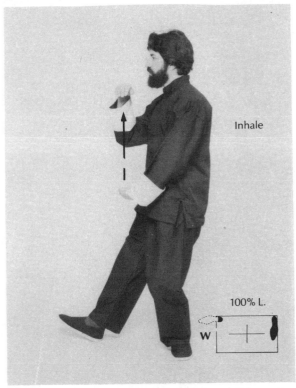

Inhale

100% L.

W

Turn 90° Rt.; pivot on Rt. heel; form a large ball with the hands along the center line of the body, Rt. hand on top.

8A. A's right wrist intercepts B's punch. A's right hand can grab B's wrist. His turn neutralizes the attack.

9.

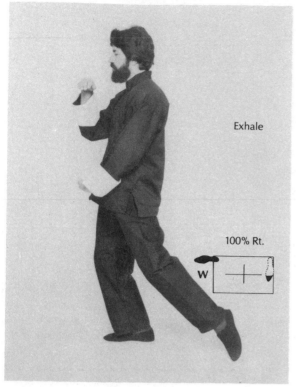

Exhale

100% Rt.

W

Shift weight Rt., lift L. heel.

10.

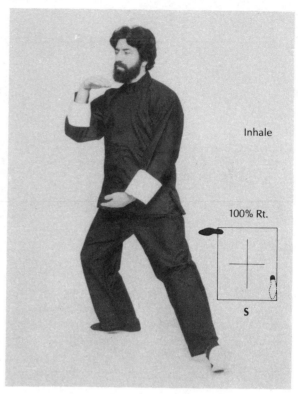

Inhale

100% Rt.

S

Turn waist L. Step forward with the L. foot to form a forward stance.

9A. A snaps B's elbow with his L. arm as he shifts forward.

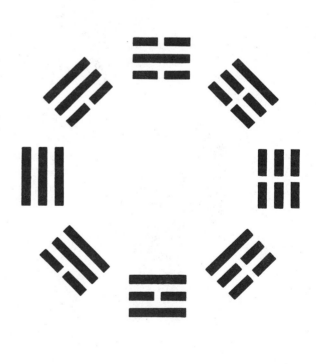

11. GRASP SPARROW'S TAIL, WARD OFF LEFT

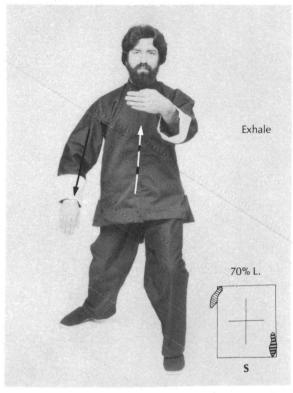

Exhale

70% L.

S

Shift weight forward. Lift back toe and turn it 45% L. as the waist turns; pivot on the Rt. heel; the L. arm rises to chest height, the Rt. arm lowers to the side of the body.

12.

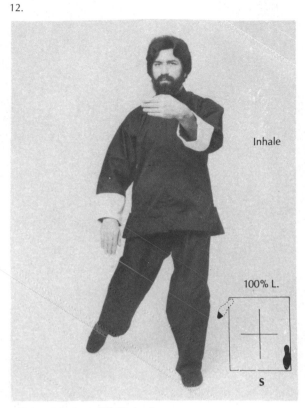

Inhale

100% L.

S

Shift weight L. and lift Rt. heel.

strikes B's elbow.

be directed

97

13.

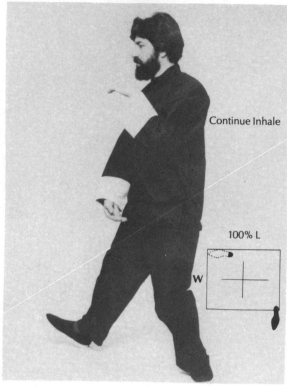

Continue Inhale

100% L

Form a ball with the hands, L. hand on top. Pivot on Rt. toe and turn 90° Rt. Lift Rt. foot and step forward to form a forward stance.

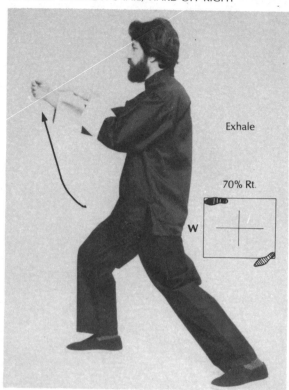

Exhale

70% Rt.

Shift weight Rt.; raise Rt. arm to chest height; lift L. toe and allow it to follow the waist 45°. L. hand points into Rt. palm which is facing the chest.

...ed for blocking. A's L. hand is used for

14B. A pulls B's Rt. arm a...

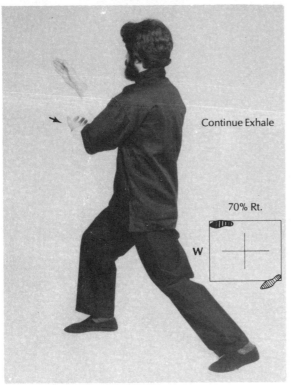

Continue Exhale

70% Rt.

W

Turn waist 45° Rt.; the L. palm goes under the Rt. forearm.

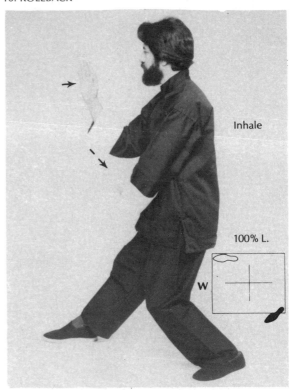

Inhale

100% L.

W

Shift weight back, lower L. palm under Rt. elbow.

15A. A's turn deflects B's punch. A attacks B's throat with his fingers.

16A. A's Rt. arm intercepts B's punch. A shifts his weight back and turns to neutralize it.

17. ROLLBACK

Continue Inhale

100% L.

Turn waist L.; lower L. arm circling it to the L. shoulder.

18. PRESS

Exhale

70% Rt.

W

Shift forward and press hands together. The heels of the palms contact each other.

18A. A shifts his weight forward to press into B's chest.

100

19. SEPARATE HANDS

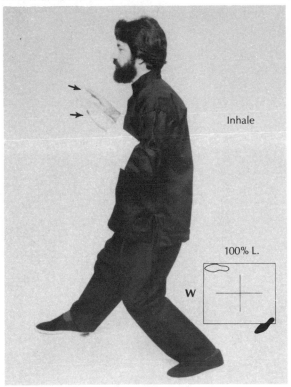

Inhale

100% L.

W

Shift weight L. and separate hands to both sides of the chest.

20. PUSH

Exhale

70% Rt.

W

Shift weight forward and push. Arms are parallel.

19A. A punch to the chest can be deflected by either or both arms.

20A. A shifts forward and attacks B's chest or throat.

21. SINGLE WHIP

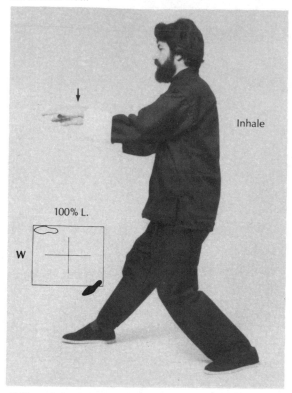

Inhale

100% L.

W

Shift weight back, lower forearms until they are parallel to the ground. Arms are ¾ extended.

22. SINGLE WHIP

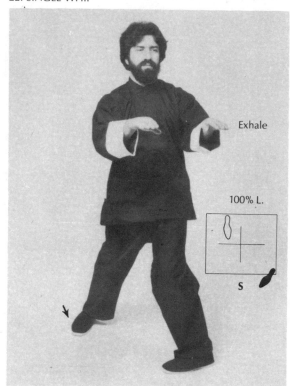

Exhale

100% L.

S

Turn 90° L., Rt. toe follows the waist. Pivot on Rt. heel.

21A. A shifts his weight back and covers B's punch, deflecting the power from it.

22A. A turns L., deflects B's punch with his L. arm, and attacks B's throat with his Rt. hand.

23. SINGLE WHIP

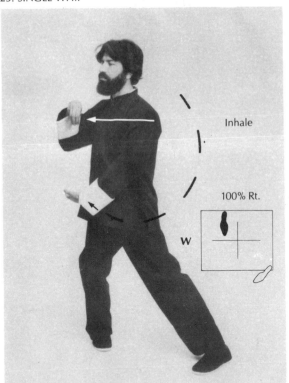

Inhale

100% Rt.

W

Form a "Crane's Beak" with the Rt. hand; shift weight Rt., turn the waist Rt. The Rt. hand goes from L. shoulder to Rt. shoulder. The L. palm faces up and is centered.

24. SINGLE WHIP

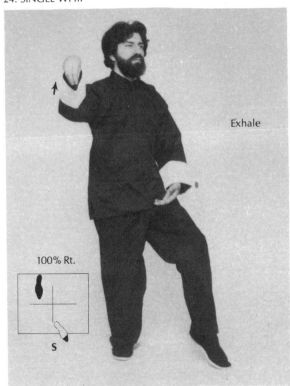

Exhale

100% Rt.

S

Lift the L. heel, turn L. and extend the Rt. wrist; pivot on L. toe.

23A. A's Rt. hand deflects B's punch. His L. arm deflects B's kick.

24A. A's L. palm deflects B's punch. A turns L., extending his "crane's beak" into B's chin.

Inhale

100% Rt

E

Step into a L. forward stance.

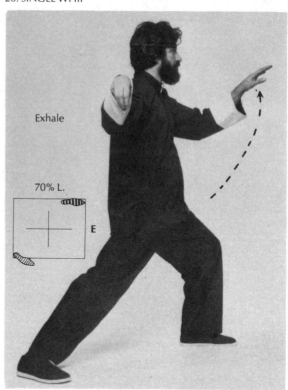

Exhale

70% L.

E

Shift weight forward and raise L. arm, point the fingers up, then turn palm away from the body. Turn Rt. toe 45° with waist.

26. Side View

26A. A turns and steps into B's punch, deflecting it and counterattacking to B's throat.

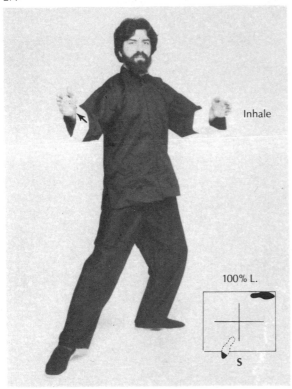

Inhale

100% L.

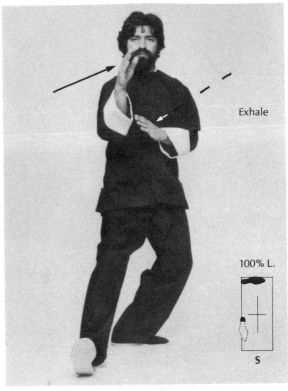

Exhale

100% L.

Raise Rt. heel, and shift weight 100% L.; turn Rt. 90°; pivot on Rt. toe.

Place Rt. heel in front of L. heel, toe up. Rt. hand protects the face, L. hand near Rt. elbow.

27A. A pulls B's L. arm and strikes B's head.

28A. A's hand is on B's wrist; A's Rt. hand is on B's elbow. A quick snap will break the elbow joint. The Rt. leg is poised to kick.

29. PULL

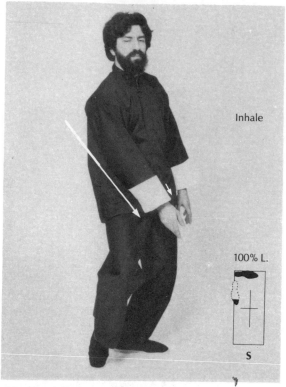

Inhale

100% L.

Bring Rt. toe back to L. heel and both hands near L. leg.

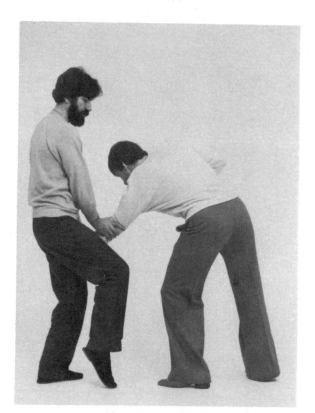

29A. As B punches, A guides and deflects his arm to the L. and down.

30. SHOULDER PRESS

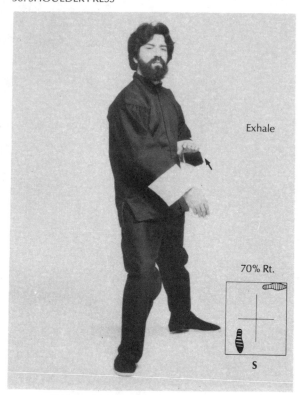

Exhale

70% Rt.

Step into a modified Rt. forward stance; Rt. arm forms a slight curve and hangs in front of the body; raise L. palm (facing down) to solar plexus height.

30A. A shifts forward and attacks B with his shoulder. A's L. hand can deflect B's punch.

Inhale

100% Rt.

E

Shift weight to Rt. leg. Place L. toe in front of Rt. heel; raise Rt. wrist palm facing away from the head; the L. arm lowers near L. leg, palm back.

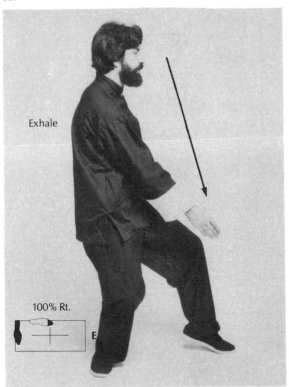

Exhale

100% Rt.

E

Lower Rt. hand, edge leading.

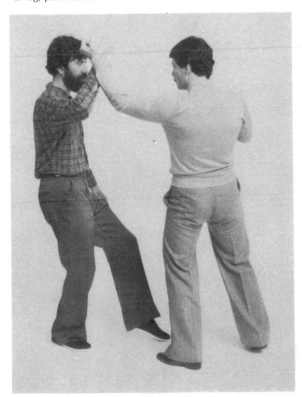

31A. A's rising Rt. arm is protecting his head. His lowering L. arm is defending against kicks. The empty front leg can kick.

32A. A's lowering Rt. hand chops B's neck or shoulder.

33.

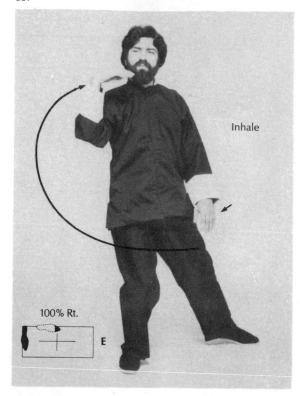

Inhale

100% Rt.

E

Turn waist Rt.; circle Rt. arm to Rt. shoulder. The L. hand moves to center.

34. BRUSH LEFT KNEE AND PUSH

Exhale

70% L.

E

Step into L. forward stance. As waist turns L., the L. palm brushes over L. knee, and the Rt. palm pushes forward; Rt. toe turns 45°.

33A. A deflects B's kick.

34A. A's L. arm deflects kicks. His Rt. arm is protecting his mid-section or countering to the chest, eyes or throat.

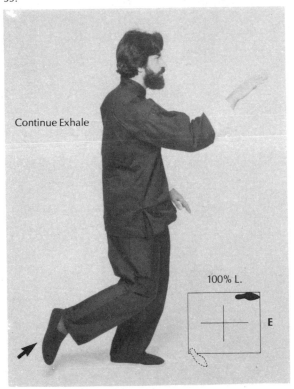

Continue Exhale

100% L.

E

Shift weight forward and lift back foot off the ground.

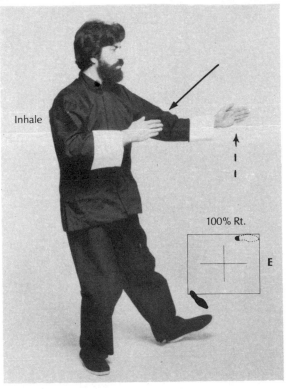

Inhale

100% Rt.

E

Place Rt. foot back down; shift weight Rt. Raise L. toe; raise L. arm; move Rt. arm Rt.

35A. A shifts forward and uproots B.

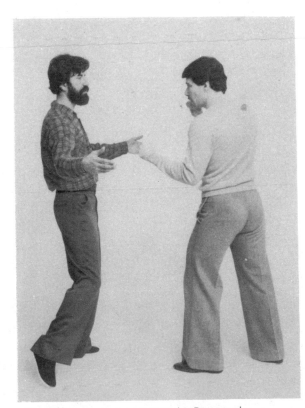

36A. A feints an opening, encouraging B. to punch.

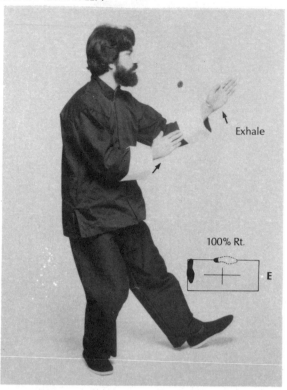

Exhale

100% Rt.

E

Lift L. foot, place L. heel in front of Rt. heel. The L. hand is in front of the face and the Rt. hand is near the L. elbow. Arms are at 45° angle.

37A. A's Rt. hand is on B's wrist; A's L. hand controls B's elbow. A quick snap will break the elbow joint.

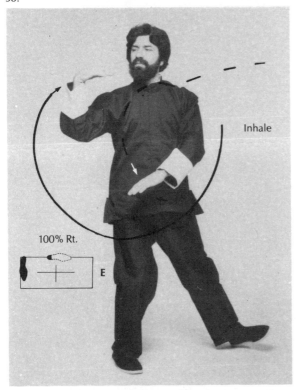

Inhale

100% Rt.

E

Lower Rt. arm; lower L. arm across chest and down. The Rt. arm circles to Rt. shoulder.

Exhale

70% L.

E

Step into L. forward stance. As waist turns L., the L. palm brushes over L. knee, and the Rt. palm pushes forward; Rt. toe turns 45°.

38A. A deflects B's punch downward.

39A. A shifts forward, striking B's eyes with his fingers.

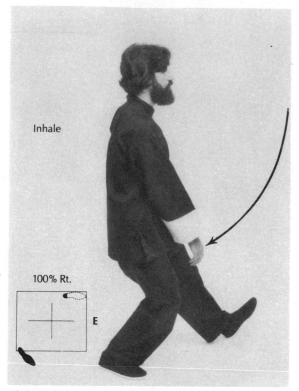

Shift weight back on to Rt. leg, lower arms and lift the L. toe.

Turn L. toe out 45°, shift forward to the L. leg, form a fist with the Rt. hand.

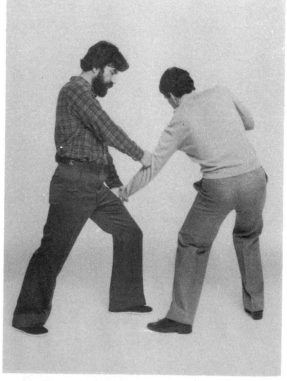

41A. A shifts forward and punches B's elbow while grabbing his wrist, breaking B's arm.

42. DEFLECT DOWNWARD

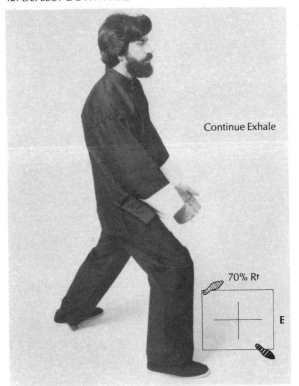

Continue Exhale

70% Rt

E

Step forward on to Rt. leg; the Rt. toe is 45° outward.

43. PARRY

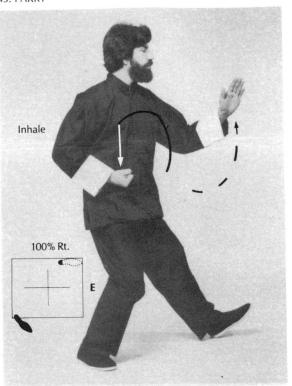

Inhale

100% Rt.

E

Bring L. heel forward, stepping into forward stance. Rt. forearm and fist cross the chest to the Rt. shoulder, then are pulled down near the waist. The L. palm follows the fist to the center of the body.

42-43. A deflects B's punch and strikes his face.

43A. A deflects B's punch and strikes his face.

44. PUNCH

Exhale

70% L.

E

Shift weight L.; the Rt. fist punches center.

44. Side View

44A. A shifts his weight forward and punches; his left arm guards or deflects.

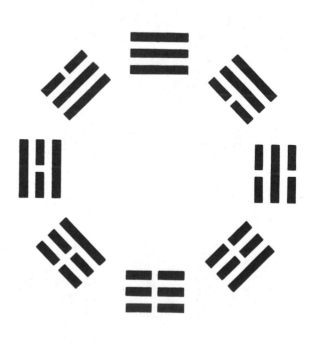

45.

46. WITHDRAW

Continue Exhale

70% L.

E

Turn waist 45° L.; place L. palm under Rt. elbow.

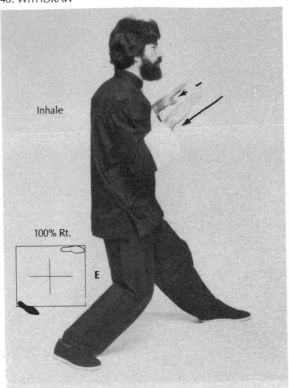

Inhale

100% Rt.

E

Open the Rt. hand, shift weight back and withdraw Rt. arm over L. hand, then both hands turn palms out.

45A. B grabs A's right arm. A's left hand comes underneath B's grasping wrist.

46A. A's left arm maintains contact with B's arm. Simultaneously, A withdraws his right arm and frees it.

47. PUSH

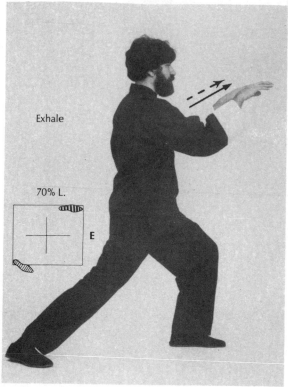

Exhale

70% L.

E

Shift weight forward and push. Arms are parallel.

48.

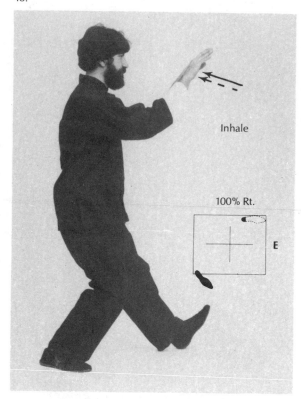

Inhale

100% Rt.

E

Shift weight back; lift L. toe. Pull arms back 45° to the chest.

47A. A shifts forward and attacks B's throat or eyes.

48A. A's arms deflect B's punches to the head or chest.

49.

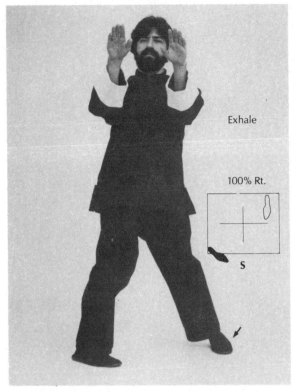

Exhale

100% Rt.

S

Turn waist 90° Rt., the L. toe follows pivoting on L. heel. Arms remain parallel.

50.

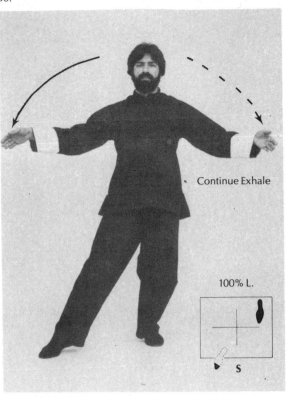

Continue Exhale

100% L.

S

Shift weight L.; raise Rt. heel; separate hands forming a large arc.

49A. A pulls B's arm and attacks B's head.

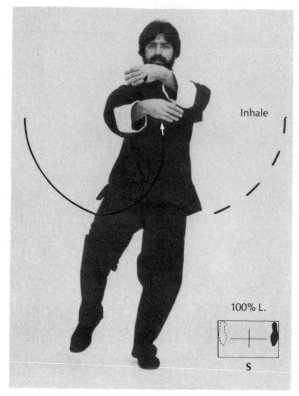

Inhale

100% L.

S

Exhale

50%-50%

S

Arms continue circling downward until they cross each other, L. wrist over Rt. (continue exhale). Arms move upward to chest height as Rt. foot is raised off the ground (inhale).

Rt. foot is placed parallel and shoulders' distance from the L. foot; the L. wrist rests on the Rt. wrist. Arms form a large circle away from the chest.

51A. A lifts both of B's arms, crossing and tangling them.

52A. A's "Cross Hands", deflect and upward punch.

The Tai Chi Form
With Applications of the Major Postures
Section II

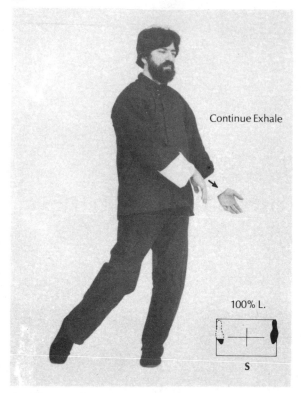

Continue Exhale

100% L.

S

Waist turns L.; lower Rt. arm. L. wrist slides down back of Rt. hand and off the middle finger.

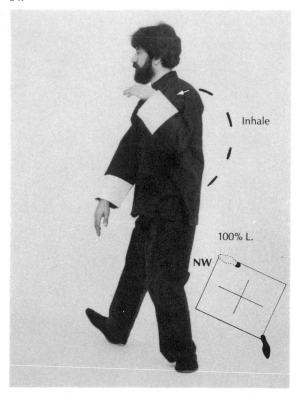

Inhale

100% L.

NW

Turn waist Rt.; circle L. arm to L. shoulder. Place Rt. heel to form a forward stance. (NW)

53A. When B grabs A's Rt. wrist, A brushes it off with his L. wrist.

54A. A deflects B's kick.

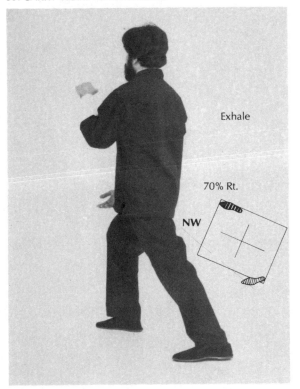

Exhale

70% Rt.

NW

Shift weight forward, brush Rt. knee with Rt. palm. Turn Rt. palm upward facing L. palm.

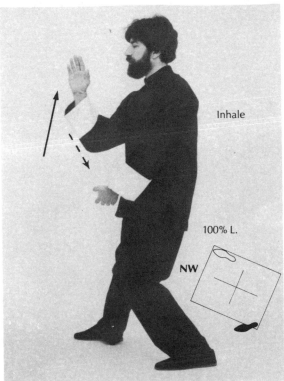

Inhale

100% L.

NW

Shift weight back raising Rt. hand as L. hand moves under Rt. wrist, arm, and elbow.

55A. A strikes B's chest and throat, while still holding B's leg.

56A. A bends B's wrist back and break's B's arm.

57. PRESS

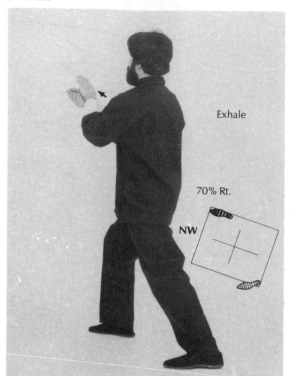

Exhale

70% Rt.

NW

Circle L. arm to L. shoulder (inhale). Shift weight forward, press palms together (exhale).

57A. A presses into B's chest.

58. SEPARATE HANDS

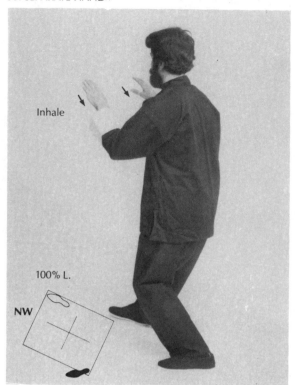

Inhale

100% L.

NW

Shift weight L. and separate hands to both sides of the chest.

58A. A deflects B's Rt. punch and strikes at B's throat with his Rt. fingertips.

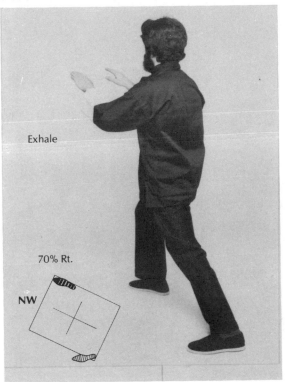

Exhale

70% Rt.

NW

Shift weight forward and push. Arms are parallel.

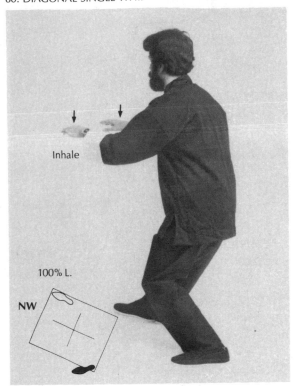

Inhale

100% L.

NW

Shift weight back, lower forearms until they are parallel to the ground. Arms are ¾ extended.

59A. A pushes B.

60A. A deflects B's L. punch downward.

61. DIAGONAL SINGLE WHIP

Exhale

100% L.

NW

Turn 90° L., Rt. toe follows the waist. Pivot on Rt. heel.

62. DIAGONAL SINGLE WHIP

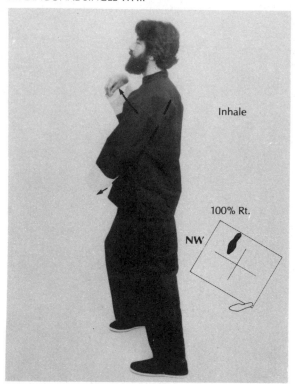

Inhale

100% Rt.

NW

Form a "Crane's Beak" with the Rt. hand; shift weight Rt., turn the waist Rt. The Rt. hand goes from L. shoulder to Rt. shoulder. The L. palm faces up and is centered.

61A. A grasps B's L. wrist and break's B's elbow.

62A. A pulls B's L. wrist down and Rt.

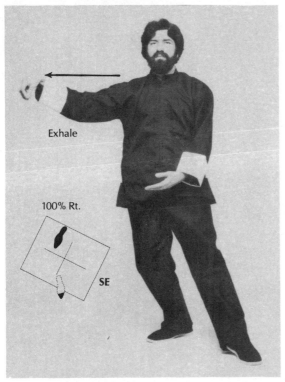

Exhale

100% Rt.

SE

Lift the L. heel, turn L. and extend the Rt. wrist; pivot on L. toe.

Inhale

100% Rt.

SE

Step into a L. forward stance.

63A. A strikes B's chin with his wrist and deflects B's punch with his forearm.

125

65. DIAGONAL SINGLE WHIP

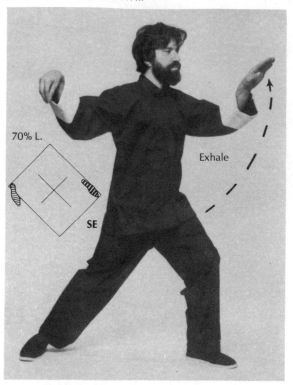

70% L.

SE

Exhale

Shift weight forward and raise L. arm, point the fingers up, then turn palm away from the body. Turn Rt. toe 45° with waist.

66.

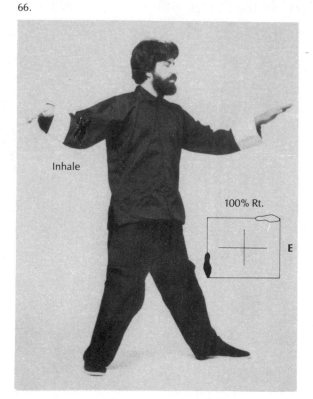

Inhale

100% Rt.

E

Shift weight to Rt. leg; open Rt. hand. Lift L. foot, turn waist L., place L. foot down. (E)

66A. A deflects B's punch.

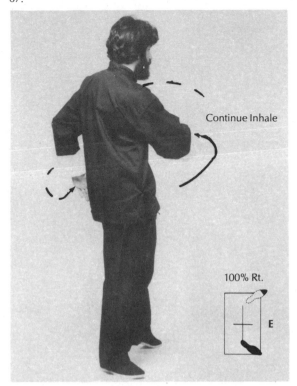

Continue Inhale

100% Rt.

E

Place Rt. foot Rt. of L. foot (SE). Shift weight 100% Rt., lift L. heel, turn waist L. as both palms push L. L. arm circles to L. waist; Rt. hand forms a fist in front of L. hip.

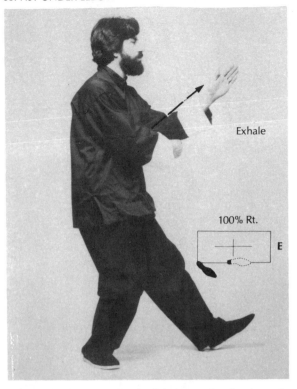

Exhale

100% Rt.

E

Place L. heel in front of Rt. heel; L. fingers, hand, arm, and elbow travel over Rt. fist at 45° angle to body.

67A. A's Rt. palm deflects B's L. punch.

68A. A grasps B's L. wrist; spears B's throat and kicks his shin.

68. Side View

69.

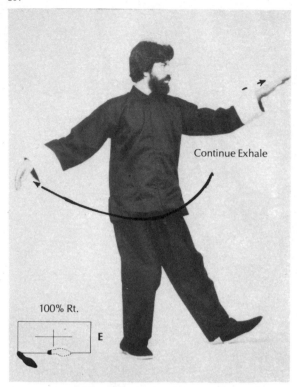

Continue Exhale

100% Rt.

E

Turn waist Rt.; drop Rt. arm and circle it toward Rt. shoulder; extend L. hand.

69A. A's L. forearm deflects B's Rt. punch. A's fingers attack B's throat.

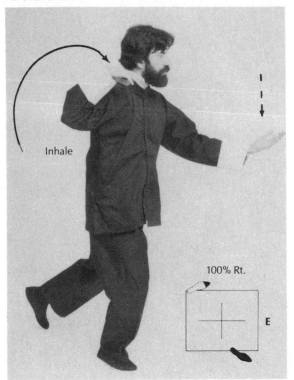

Circle Rt. hand to Rt. shoulder; turn L. palm up, place L. toe back.

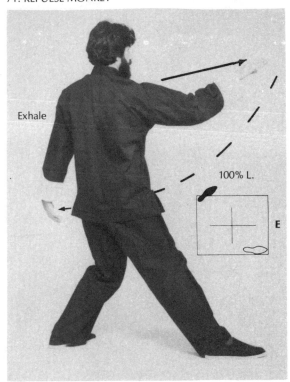

Shift weight back to L. foot; turn waist L.; turn Rt. toe E. Drop the L. arm; extend Rt. arm.

69B. A deflects B's punch downward while attacking the eyes.

71. Side View.

72. STEP BACK

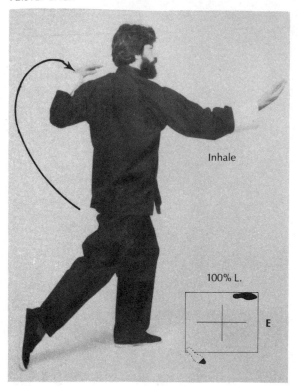

Inhale

100% L.

E

Circle L. hand to L. shoulder. Turn Rt. palm up, place Rt. toe back.

73. REPULSE MONKEY

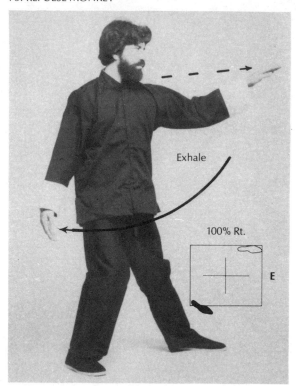

Exhale

100% Rt.

E

Shift weight to Rt. foot, and turn waist Rt. Turn L. toe E.; drop Rt. arm; extend L. hand.

73. Side View.

73A. A's L. forearm deflects B's Rt. punch. A's fingers attach B's throat.

74. STEP BACK

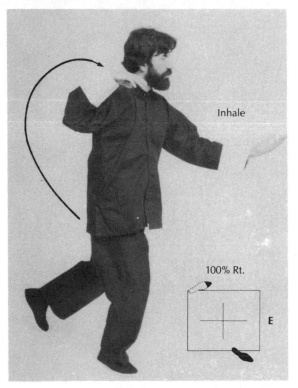

Inhale

100% Rt.

E

Circle Rt. hand to Rt. shoulder; turn L. palm up, place L. toe back.

75. REPULSE MONKEY

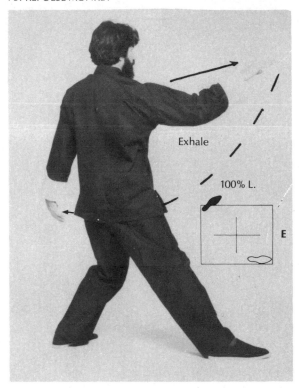

Exhale

100% L.

E

Shift weight back to L. foot; turn waist L.; turn Rt. toe E. Drop the L. arm; extend Rt. arm.

75A. A's L. arm deflects B's kick. A's Rt. hand attacks B's throat.

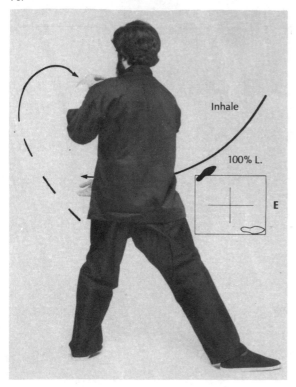

Circle L. arm to L. shoulder, palm down; drop Rt. hand to form a ball.

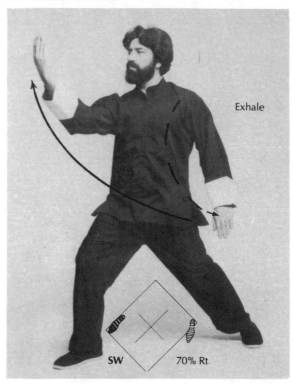

Lift Rt. foot and step clockwise into a forward stance (SW). Shift weight Rt. and allow L. toe to follow waist, pivot on L. heel; Rt. arm circles to head height in front of Rt. shoulder. L. arm drops down, palm facing back.

77A. A grasps B's wrist and attacks B's head and throat.

78.

Inhale

100% Rt.

SW

Shift weight Rt.; turn waist Rt.; form a ball, Rt. hand on top; lift L. heel.

79.

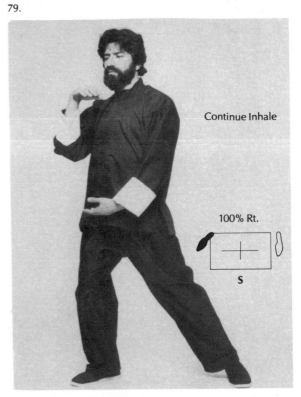

Continue Inhale

100% Rt.

S

Step up with L. foot (S).

77B. A grabs B's kick and attacks the groin.

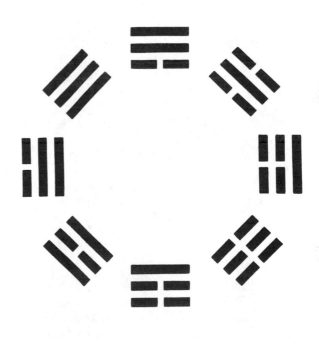

Exhale

100% L.

S

Shift weight L.; lower Rt. hand; raise L. hand to chest height.

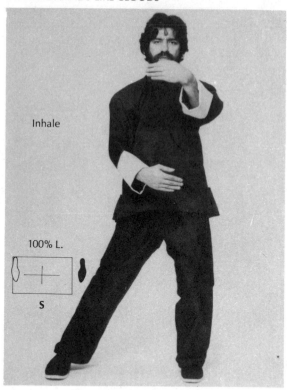

Inhale

100% L.

S

Turn waist L., Rt. toe follows until both feet face S. L. palm faces the chest, Rt. palm faces the Tan Tien.

80A. A deflects B's kicks.

81A. A deflects a kick and a punch.

82. WAVE HANDS LIKE CLOUDS

Continue Inhale

100% L.

S

Turn waist 90° L. and form a ball, L. hand on top.

83. WAVE HANDS LIKE CLOUDS

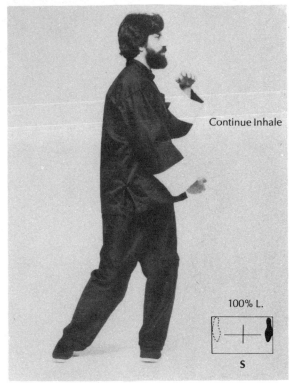

Continue Inhale

100% L.

S

Lift Rt. foot and step closer together keeping feet parallel.

82A. A deflects B's kick and holds his leg.

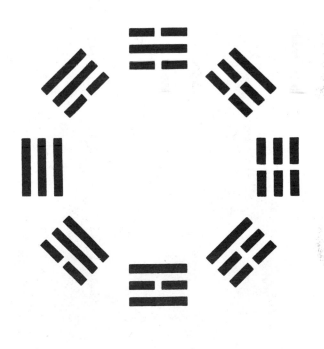

135

84. WAVE HANDS LIKE CLOUDS

Exhale

100% Rt.

S

Shift weight Rt.; lower L. hand; raise Rt. hand to chest height.

85. WAVE HANDS LIKE CLOUDS

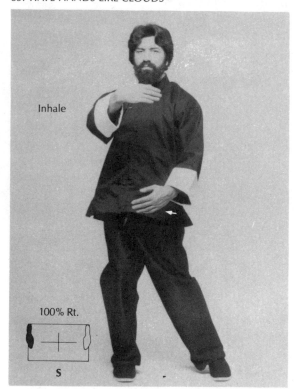

Inhale

100% Rt.

S

Turn waist 90° Rt., palm faces chest, L. palm faces Tan Tien.

84A. A deflects B's kick.

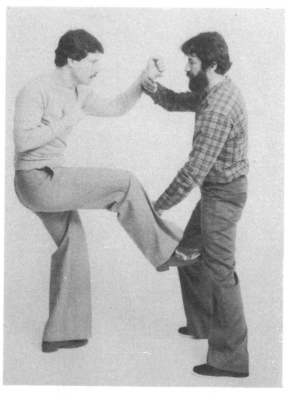

85A. A deflects a kick and a punch.

86. WAVE HANDS LIKE CLOUDS

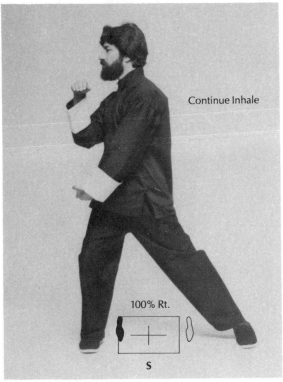

Continue Inhale

100% Rt.

S

Turn waist 90° Rt., hands form a ball, Rt. hand on top. Step L. with L. foot (5).

87. WAVE HANDS LIKE CLOUDS

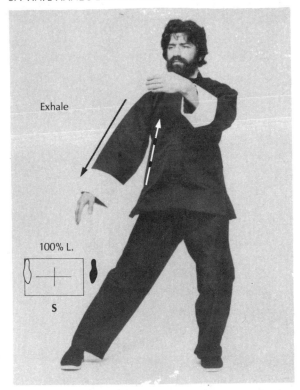

Exhale

100% L.

S

Shift weight L.; lower Rt. hand; raise L. hand to chest height.

87A. A deflects B's kick.

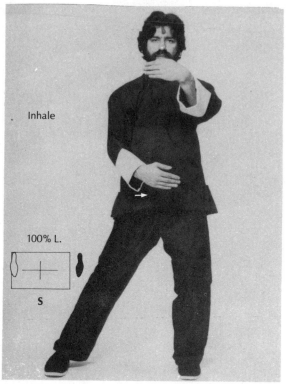

Inhale

100% L.

S

Turn waist L., L. palm faces the chest, Rt. palm faces the Tan Tien.

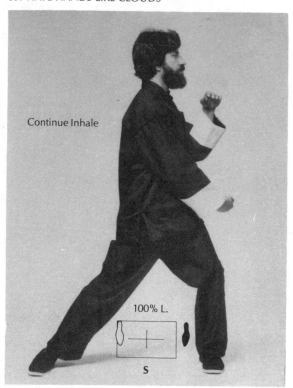

Continue Inhale

100% L.

S

Turn waist 90° L. and form a ball, L. hand on top.

88A. A deflects a kick and a punch.

89A. A deflects B's kick and holds his leg.

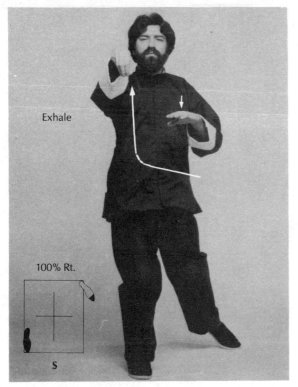

Exhale

100% Rt.

S

Step up with R. foot (S). Shift weight Rt.; raise L. heel, turn waist 90° Rt.; Rt. wrist forms a "Crane's Beak" and comes up in front of Rt. shoulder.

Exhale

70% L.

E

Turn waist 90° L.; pivot on L. toe. Lift L. toe and place L. heel to form a forward stance (E) (inhale). Shift weight L.; bring L. hand up; turn palm E; Rt. toe follows waist 45° L. (exhale).

90A. A's Rt. arm deflects a punch. A's wrist attacks B's head.

91A. A turns and steps into B's punch, deflecting it and counterattacking to B's throat.

93.

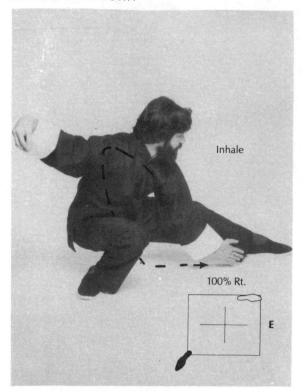

Inhale

100% Rt.

E

Turn Rt. toe SW, shift weight 70% Rt.; L. toe turns S; bring L. hand near Rt. knee; squat down, weight 100% on Rt. foot, let L. hand drop near the Rt. foot, and move toward the L. foot. Turn L. toe E.

Exhale

70% L.

E

Shift weight L., raise body and L. hand to chest height; lower Rt. arm. Rt. toe follows waist 45°. Open Rt. hand.

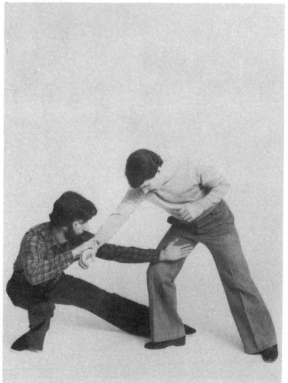

92A. A pulls B's arm downward and attacks B's groin.

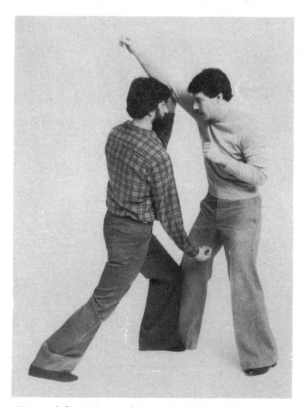

93A. A deflects B's punch upward and attacks B's groin.

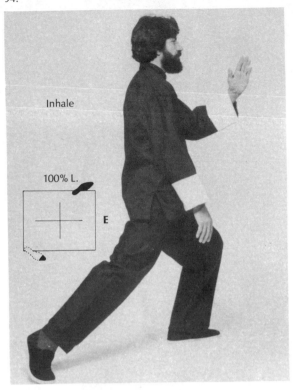

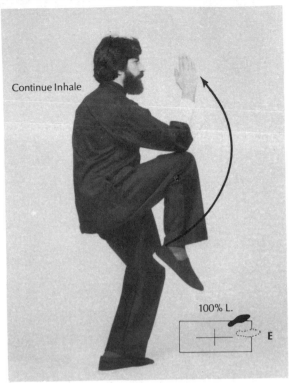

Turn L. toe 45°NE, raise Rt. heel.

Raise Rt. knee and Rt. arm forming a continuous line in front of the body. Lower L. arm palm back, near L. leg.

94A. A deflects a punch and intercepts a kick.

95A. A's arm deflects a punch. A's knee deflects a kick.

96.

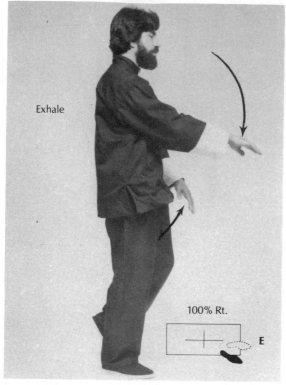

Exhale

100% Rt.

E

Lower Rt. arm and leg, toe facing SE; start lifting L. arm and heel.

97. GOLDEN PHEASANT STANDS ON ONE LEG, LEFT

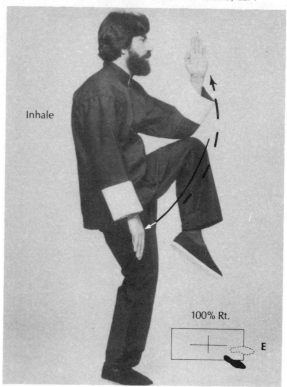

Inhale

100% Rt.

E

Raise L. knee and L. arm forming a continuous line in front of the body, lower Rt. arm, palm back, near the Rt. leg.

96A. A intercepts a kick and a punch.

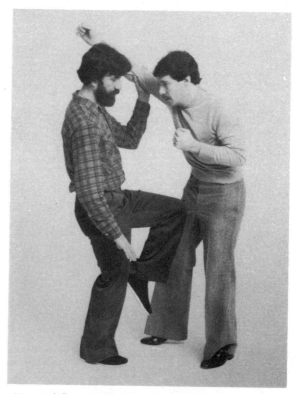

97A. A deflects B's punch upward and his knee attacks B's groin.

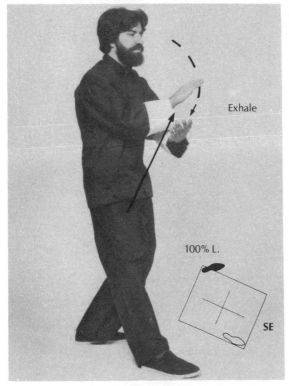

Exhale

100% L.

SE

Step back with L. foot. Look at L. palm and cross L. forearm with Rt. forearm, Rt. palm down.

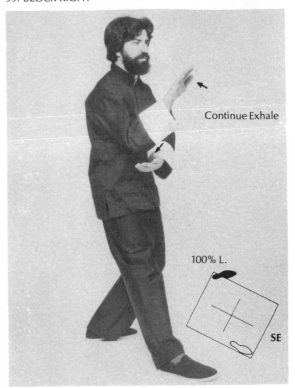

Continue Exhale

100% L.

SE

Turn waist Rt.; Rt. arm follows waist; L. palm comes under Rt. elbow.

98A. A's L. forearm deflects a punch.

99A. A's Rt. forearm deflects a punch.

100.

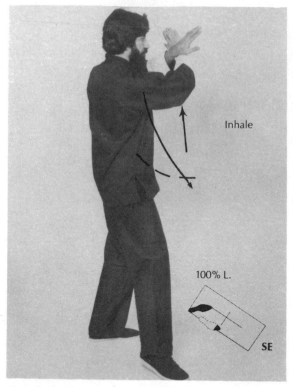

Inhale

100% L.

SE

Drop both arms; turn waist L. and allow Rt. toe to follow (NE). L. wrist crosses over Rt. wrist forming a low block (N). Raise both wrists forming a high block (N); raise Rt. heel. Turn waist Rt. and pivot on Rt. toe to SE.

101. SEPARATE RIGHT FOOT.

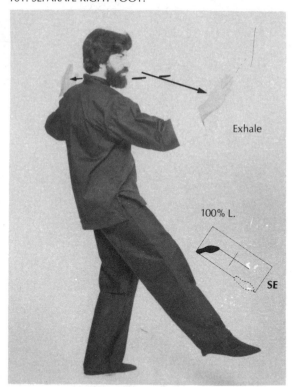

Exhale

100% L.

SE

Separate arms and Rt. foot, kicking to shin height (SE).

101A. A grasps and pulls B's wrist downward and kicks to the shin.

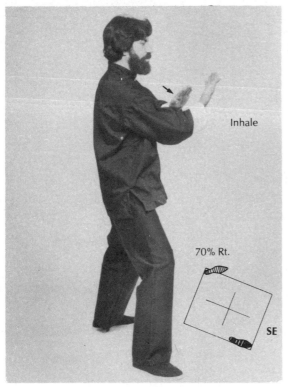

Inhale

70% Rt.

SE

Step SE into a Rt. forward stance, Rt. palm faces the head; L. arm crosses, palm down, over Rt. Elbow.

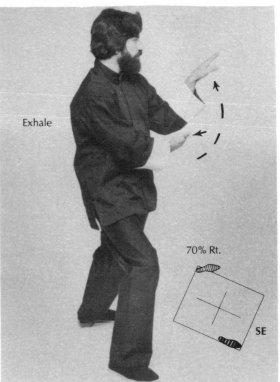

Exhale

70% Rt.

SE

Turn waist SE; L. palm faces NE; Rt. palm arrives beneath L. elbow.

103A. A's L. forearm deflects a punch.

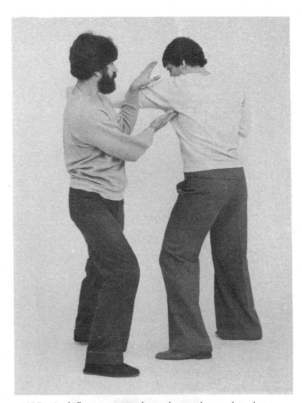

103B. A deflects a punch and attacks under the arm, simultaneously.

104.

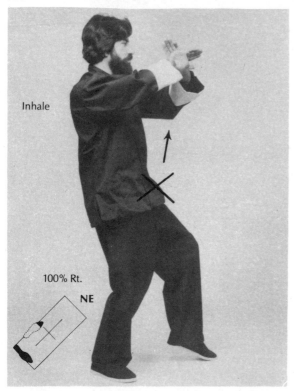

Inhale

100% Rt.

NE

Drop both arms, place L. toe in front of Rt. heel (NE). Rt. wrist crosses over L. wrist forming a low block (SE). Raise arms forming a high block (SE).

105. SEPARATE LEFT FOOT

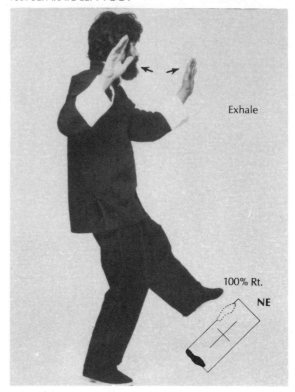

Exhale

100% Rt.

NE

Separate arms and L. foot, kicking to shin height.

104A. A's cross block deflects a punch upward.

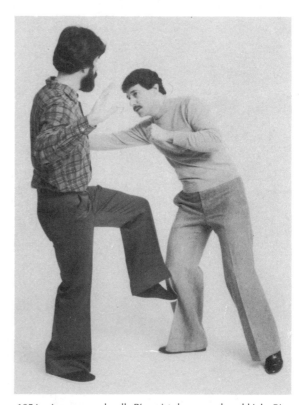

105A. A grasps and pulls B's wrist downward and kicks B's shin.

106.

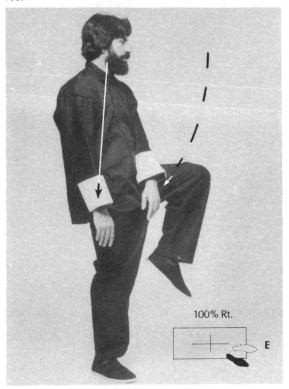

Drop both arms and raise L. knee (E).

107. TURN AROUND

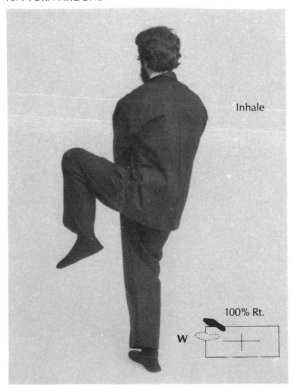

Inhale

100% Rt.

Pivot on Rt. heel, turn and cross wrists, Rt. over L., forming a low block(N); L. knee faces W.

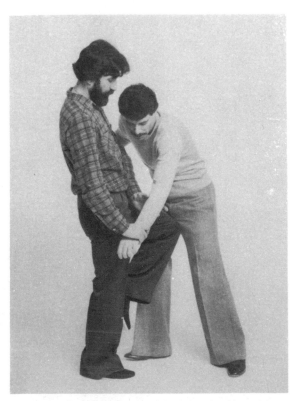

106A. A pulls B downward with both hands and attacks B's groin with his knee.

108.

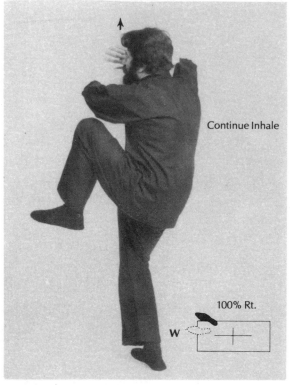

Continue Inhale

100% Rt.

W

Lift L. knee closer to chest, raise wrists forming a high block (N).

109. STRIKE WITH HEEL

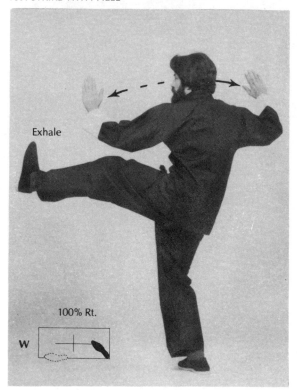

Exhale

100% Rt.

W

Extend L. leg; kick with L. heel, stomach height.

108A. A deflects a punch and a kick.

109A. A deflects a punch and kicks to the stomach.

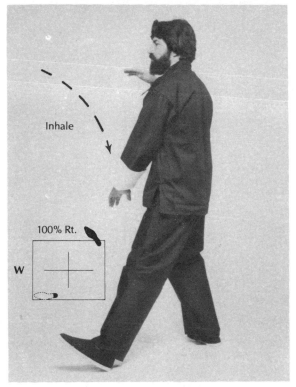

Inhale

100% Rt.

W

Drop L. shin, leave L. knee up; drop L. arm, palm facing Rt. hip. Place L. heel to form a forward stance (W).

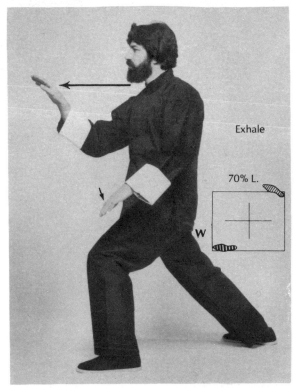

Exhale

70% L.

W

Shift forward; L. palm brushes over L. knee; Rt. hand pushes (W).

109B. A pulls B's wrist while kicking to the stomach.

111A. A catches B's kicking leg and attacks B's throat.

112.

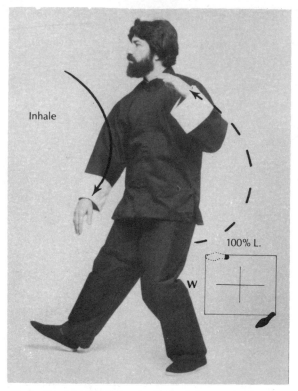

Inhale

100% L.

Turn out L. toe 45° (SW); raise Rt. heel; Rt. arm drops, palm facing L. hip. Place Rt. heel to form a forward stance (W), L. hand circles near L. shoulder.

113. BRUSH RIGHT KNEE AND PUSH

Exhale

70% Rt.

Shift forward; Rt. palm brushes over Rt. knee, L. hand pushes (W).

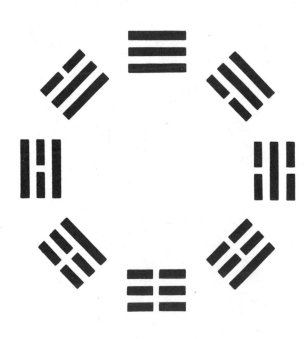

113A. A deflects B's kick and attacks his eyes.

114.

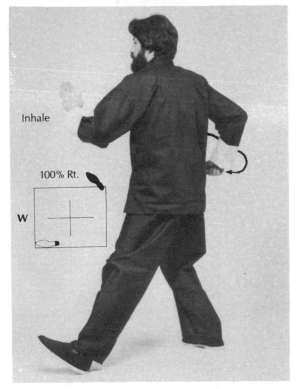

Inhale

100% Rt.

W

Turn Rt. toe out 45° (NW). Raise L. heel; shift forward. Circle Rt. hand to Rt. waist, form a fist; place L. heel to form a forward stance (W).

115. PUNCH DOWNWARD

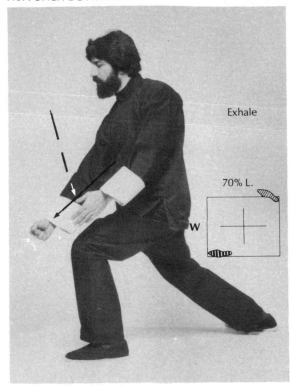

Exhale

70% L.

W

Shift weight forward and punch down to knee level, slightly Rt. of the Rt. knee.

114A. A's L. palm deflects B's Rt. punch.

115A. A shifts foreward and attacks B's groin.

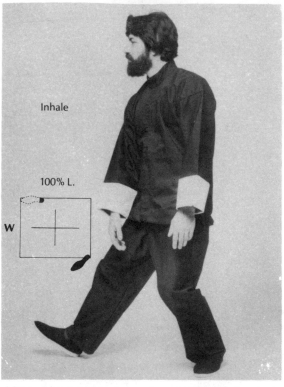

Inhale

100% L.

W

Shift weight slightly back, turn L. toe 45° (SW); drop both arms. Step with Rt. heel to form a forward stance.

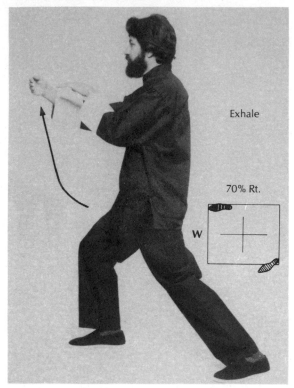

Exhale

70% Rt.

W

Shift weight forward and raise both hands, Rt. palm faces the chest; L. hand pointing into palm.

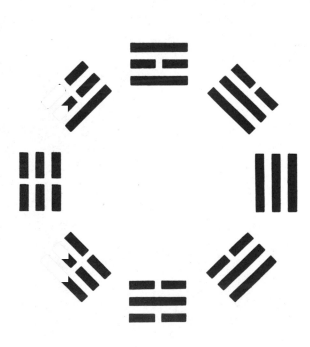

117A. A deflects B's punch with his Rt. forearm and attacks B's throat.

118. GRASP SPARROW'S TAIL, ROLLBACK

Continue Exhale

70% Rt.

W

Turn waist 45° Rt.; the L. palm goes under the Rt. forearm.

119. ROLLBACK

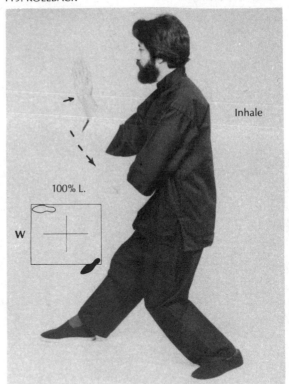

Inhale

100% L.

W

Shift weight back, lower L. palm under Rt. elbow.

119A. A pulls B's punching arm downward and can snap his elbow.

120. ROLLBACK

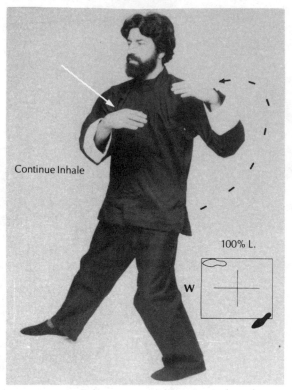

Continue Inhale

100% L.

W

Turn waist L.; lower L. arm circling it to the L. shoulder.

121. PRESS

Exhale

70% Rt.

W

Shift forward and press hands together. The heels of the palms contact each other.

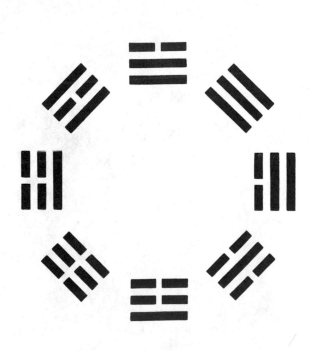

121A. A presses into B's chest and throat.

122. SEPARATE HANDS

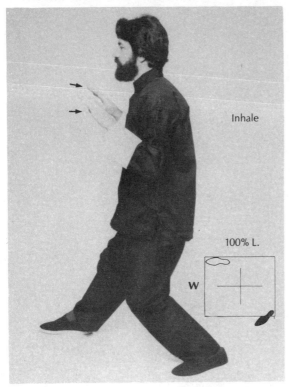

Inhale

100% L.

Shift weight L. and separate hands to both sides of the chest.

123. PUSH

Exhale

70% Rt.

W

Shift weight forward and push. Arms are parallel.

122A. A deflects two punches sumultaneously.

123A. A deflects B's punch and attacks his throat.

124. SINGLE WHIP

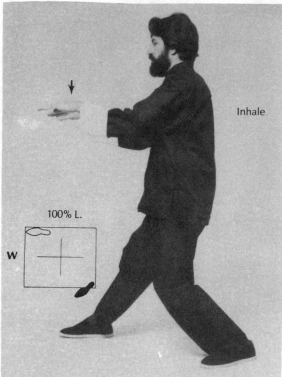

Inhale

100% L.

W

Shift weight back, lower forearms until they are parallel to the ground. Arms are ¾ extended.

125. SINGLE WHIP

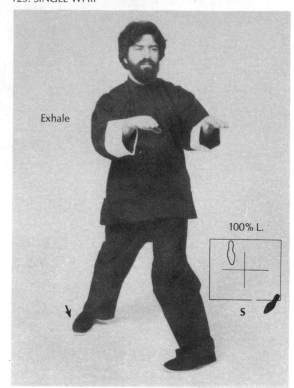

Exhale

100% L.

S

Turn 90° L., Rt. toe follows the waist. Pivot on Rt. heel.

124A. A shifts his weight back and covers B's punch, deflecting the power from it.

125A. A turns to deflect B's kick.

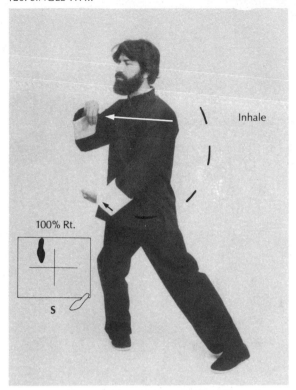

Form a "Crane's Beak" with the Rt. hand; shift weight Rt., turn the waist Rt. The Rt. hand goes from L. shoulder to Rt. shoulder; The L. palm faces up and is centered.

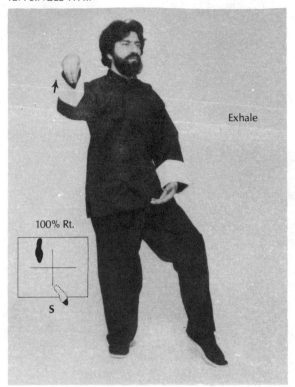

Lift the L. heel, turn L. and extend the Rt. wrist; pivot on L. toe.

126A. A pulls B's arm and attacks his throat.

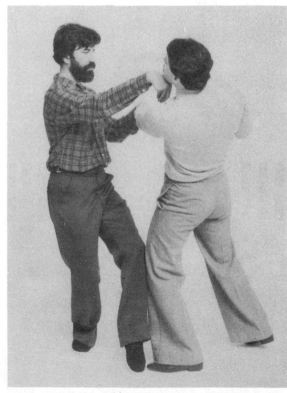

127A. A's L. palm deflects B's punch. A turns L., extending his "Crane's Beak" into B's chin.

128. SINGLE WHIP

Inhale

100% Rt.

E

Step into a L. forward stance.

129. SINGLE WHIP

Exhale

70% L.

E

Shift weight forward and raise L. arm, point the fingers up, then turn palm away from the body. Turn Rt. toe 45° with waist.

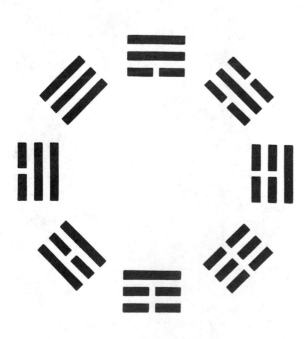

129A. A turns and steps into B's punch, deflecting it and counterattacking to B's throat.

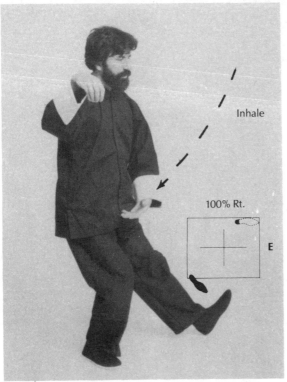

Inhale

100% Rt.

E

Shift weight to Rt. foot, raise L. toe. Bring L. palm to center of body.

Continue Inhale

100% Rt.

S

Turn waist Rt., L. toe follows to Rt.

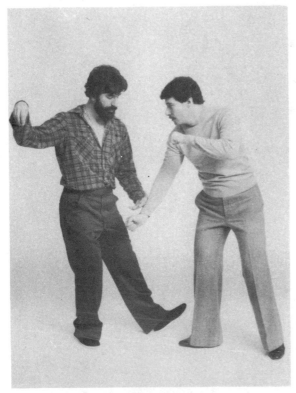

130A. A deflects B's punch downward.

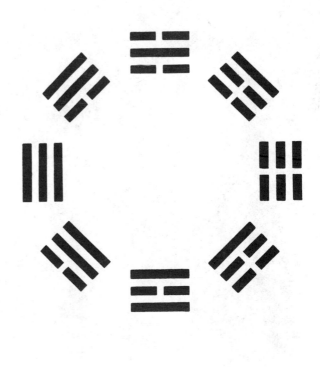

132. FOUR CORNERS

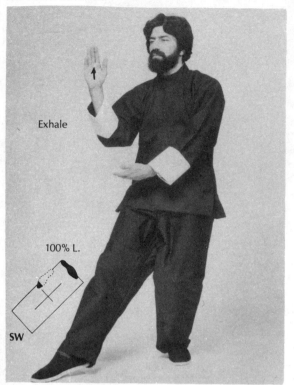

Exhale

100% L.

SW

Shift weight L., raise Rt. heel, body facing SW. Drop Rt. elbow and bring Rt. hand in front of Rt. shoulder, palm facing L.

133. FOUR CORNERS

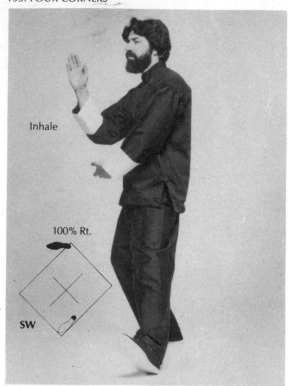

Inhale

100% Rt.

SW

Step out with the Rt. foot (NW). Shift weight Rt. Place L. heel to form a forward stance (SW).

132A. As A turns to step he simultaneously blocks B's punch.

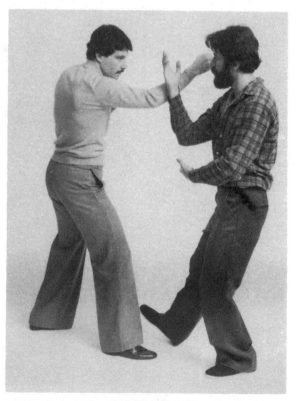

132B. As A turns to step he simultantously blocks B's punch.

160

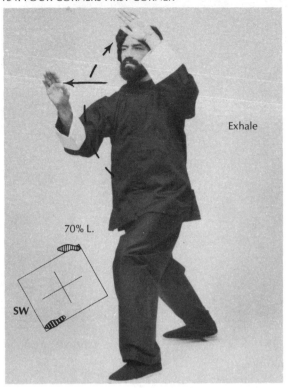

Exhale

70% L.

SW

Shift weight forward; L. arm raises to form a high block; Rt. arm pushes forward.

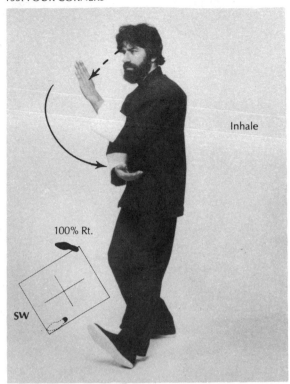

Inhale

100% Rt.

SW

Shift weight to Rt. foot; raise L. toe; lower L. elbow and bring L. hand closer to the body; Rt. palm comes to L. ribcage.

134A. A deflects a punch and attacks B's chest.

161

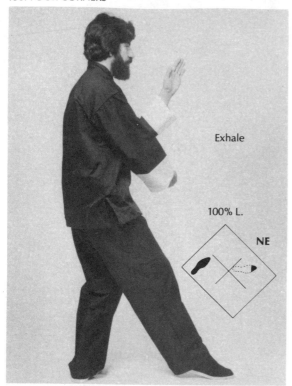

Exhale

100% L.

NE

Turn waist to Rt.; L. toe follows (continue inhale). Shift weight to L. foot; raise the Rt. heel, continue turning waist Rt. (exhale).

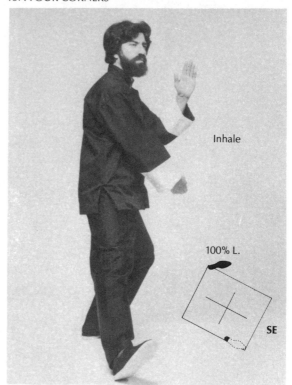

Inhale

100% L.

SE

Place Rt. heel to form a forward stance (SE).

136A. A prepares to deflect B's punch.

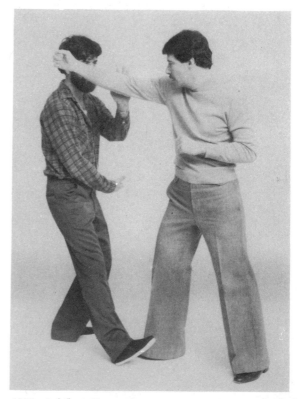

137A. A deflects B's punch.

138. FOUR CORNERS-SECOND CORNER

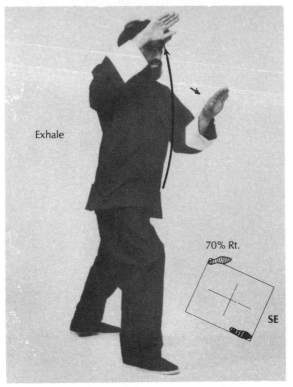

Exhale

70% Rt.

SE

Shift forward; Rt. arm rises to form a high block; L. arm pushes forward.

139. FOUR CORNERS

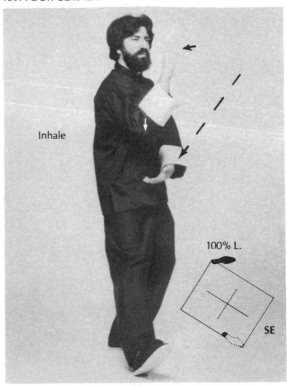

Inhale

100% L.

SE

Shift weight to L. foot; raise Rt. toe; lower Rt. elbow and bring Rt. hand closer to body; L. palm comes to Rt. ribcage.

138A. A deflects B's high punch and attacks his ribs.

140. FOUR CORNERS

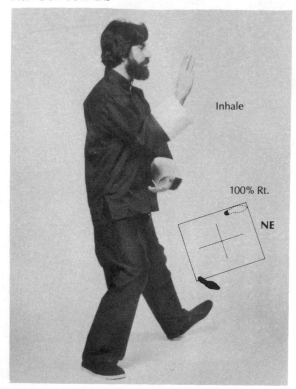

Inhale

100% Rt.

NE

Lift and place Rt. foot across L. foot, toe facing SE (exhale). Shift weight Rt. Place L. heel to form a forward stance NE (inhale).

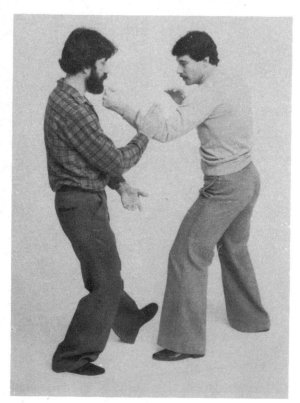

140A. A deflects B's L. punch.

141. FOUR CORNERS-THIRD CORNER

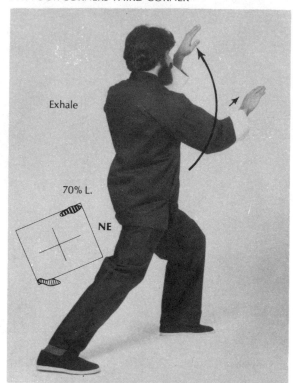

Exhale

70% L.

NE

Shift forward; left arm rises to form a high block; Rt. arm pushes forward.

141A. A deflects B's punch upward and attacks his ribs.

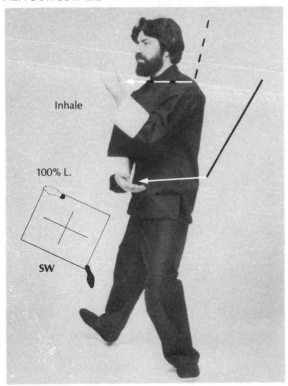

Inhale

100% L.

SW

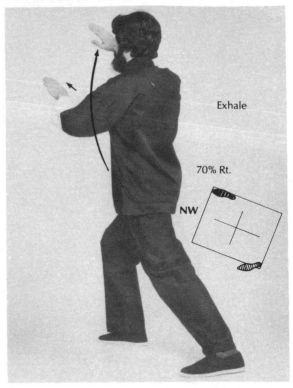

Exhale

70% Rt.

NW

Shift weight 100% Rt.; lower L. elbow and bring L. hand closer to body. Rt. palm comes to L. ribcage (inhale). Turn waist Rt.; L. toe follows (S) (continue inhale). Shift weight to L. foot; raise the Rt. heel, continue turning waist Rt. (SW) (exhale). Place L. heel to form a forward stance (NW) (inhale).

Shift forward; Rt. arm rises to form a high block; L. arm pushes forward (NW).

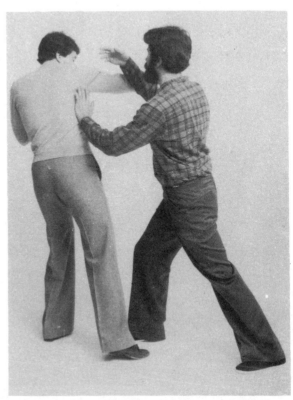

143A. A deflects B's punch to the Rt. and attacks B's ribs.

144.

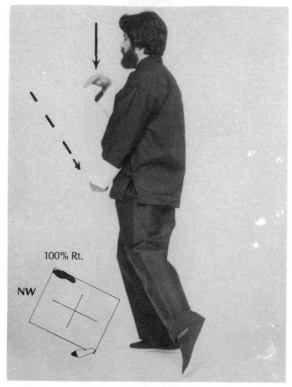

Shift weight forward, lift L. heel; drop arms to form a ball, Rt. hand on top.

145.

Inhale

Turn waist L., pivoting on L. toe. Place L. heel to form a forward stance.

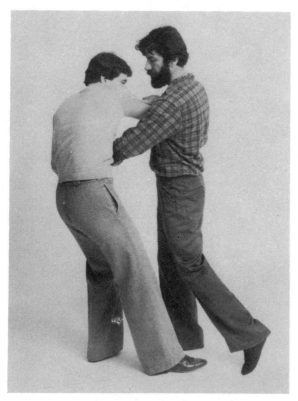

144A. A grasps B's Rt. arm and attacks his stomach.

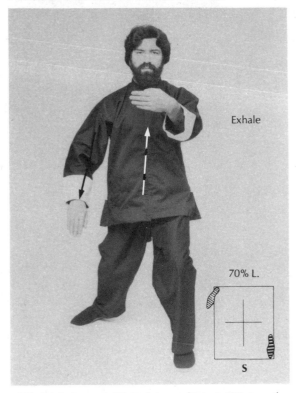

Exhale

70% L.

S

Shift weight forward. Lift back toe and turn it 45% L. as the waist turns; pivot on the Rt. heel; the L. arm rises to chest height, the Rt. arm lowers to the side of the body.

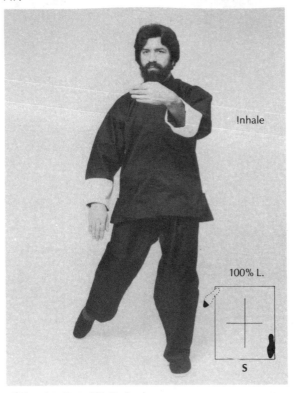

Inhale

100% L.

S

Shift weight L. and lift Rt. heel.

146A. A grasps B's wrist and attacks his throat.

148.

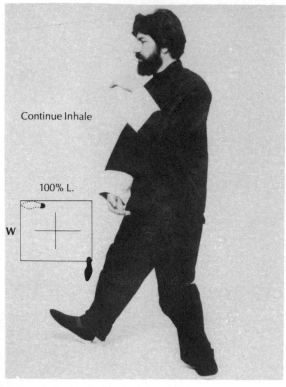

Continue Inhale

100% L.

W

Form a ball with the hands, L. hand on top. Pivot on Rt. toe and turn 90° Rt. Lift Rt. foot and step forward to form a forward stance.

149. GRASP SPARROW'S TAIL, WARD OFF, RIGHT

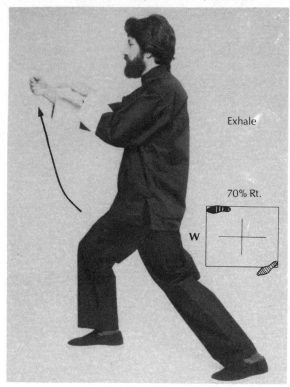

Exhale

70% Rt.

W

Shift weight Rt.; raise Rt. arm to chest height; lift L. toe and allow it to follow the waist 45°. L. hand points into Rt. palm which is facing the chest.

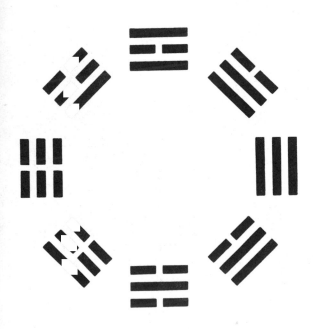

149A. A deflects B's L. arm.

Continue Exhale

70% Rt.

W

Turn waist 45° Rt.; the L. palm goes under the Rt. forearm.

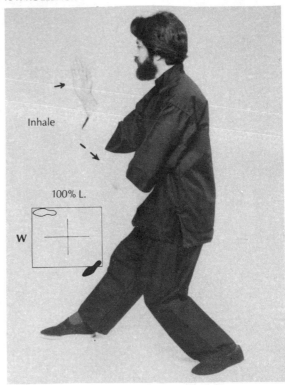

Inhale

100% L.

W

Shift weight back, lower L. palm under Rt. elbow.

149B. A's L. hand parries a punch while his Rt. hand attacks the face.

151A. A grabs B's wrist and hammers B's elbow.

152. ROLLBACK

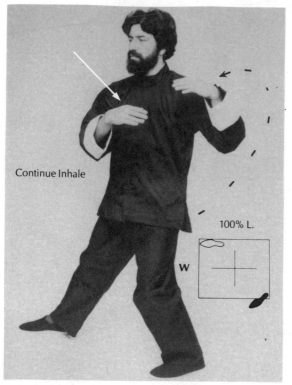

Continue Inhale

100% L.

W

Turn waist L.; lower L. arm circling it to the L. shoulder.

153. PRESS

Exhale

70% Rt.

W

Shift forward and press hands together. The heels of the palms contact each other.

152A. A deflects B's punch downward.

153A. A presses into B's chin.

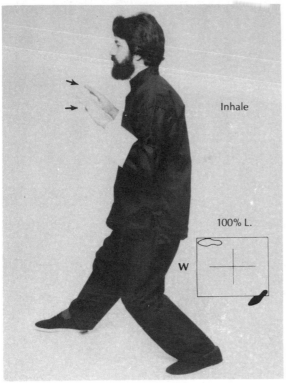

Inhale

100% L.

Shift weight L. and separate hands to both sides of the chest.

Exhale

70% Rt.

Shift weight forward and push. Arms are parallel.

154A. A punch to the chest can be deflected by either or both arms.

155A. A strikes B's eyes.

156. SINGLE WHIP

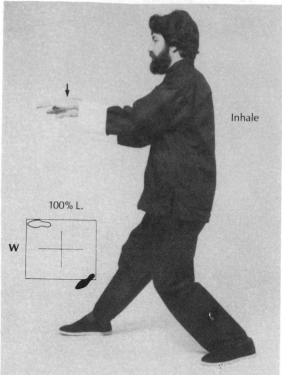

Inhale

100% L.

W

Shift weight back, lower forearms until they are parallel to the ground. Arms are ¾ extended.

157. SINGLE WHIP

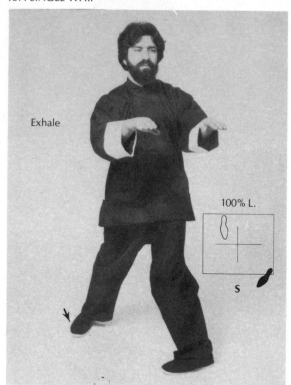

Exhale

100% L.

S

Turn 90° L., Rt. toe follows the waist. Pivot on Rt. heel.

156A. A shifts his weight back and covers B's punch, deflecting the power from it.

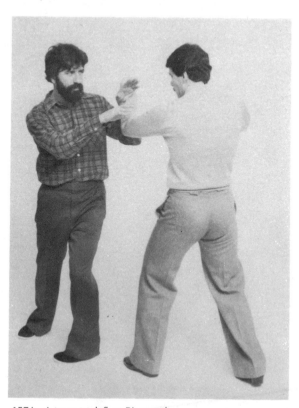

157A. A turns to deflect B's punch.

Inhale

100% Rt.

S

Form a "Crane's Beak" with the Rt. hand; shift weight Rt., turn the waist Rt. The Rt. hand goes from L. shoulder to Rt. shoulder. The L. palm faces up and is centered.

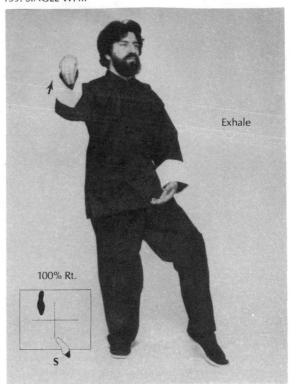

Exhale

100% Rt.

S

Lift the L. heel, turn L. and extend the Rt. wrist; pivot on L. toe.

158A. A's "crane's beak" holds B's wrist while A's upper arm snaps B's elbow.

159A. A's L. hand deflects B's punch while A's "crane's beak" attacks B's eye.

160. SINGLE WHIP

Inhale

100% Rt.

E

Step into a L. forward stance.

161. SINGLE WHIP

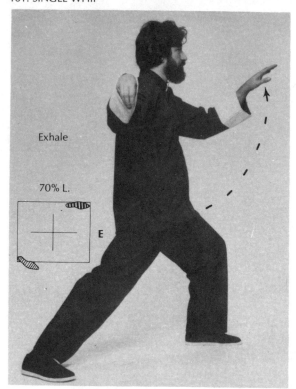

Exhale

70% L.

E

Shift weight forward and raise L. arm, point the fingers up, then turn palm away from the body. Turn Rt. toe 45° with waist.

161A. A turns and steps into B's punch, deflecting it and counterattacking to B's throat.

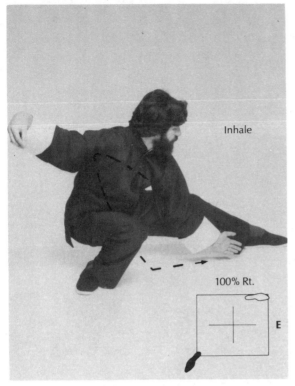

Inhale

100% Rt.

E

Turn Rt. toe SW, shift weight 70% Rt.; L. toe turns S; bring L. hand near Rt. knee; squat down, weight 100% on Rt. foot and let L. hand drop near the Rt. foot, move toward the L. foot. Turn L. toe E.

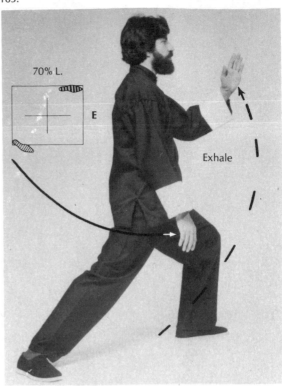

70% L.

E

Exhale

Shift weight L., raise body and L. hand to chest height; lower Rt. arm. Rt. toe follows waist 45°. Open Rt. hand.

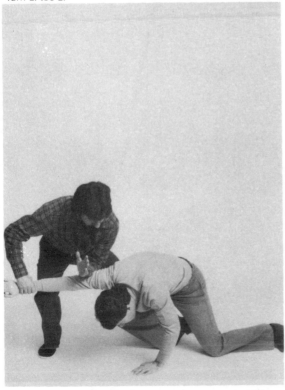

162A. A grabs B's Rt. wrist, squats, pulling B to the ground. A's L. arm snaps B's elbow.

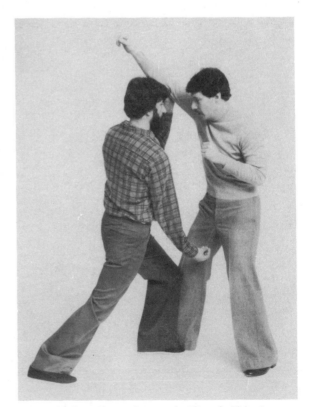

163A. A deflects B's punch upward and attacks B's groin.

164. STEP FORWARD TO SEVEN STARS

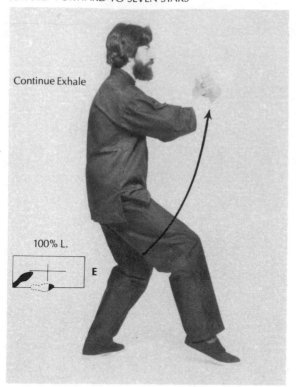

Turn out L. toe 45°; place Rt. toe in front of L. heel; form two fists and cross wrist in front of chest, 45° angle to body, L. over Rt.

164A. A's cross block deflects a high punch upward; A kicks to B's shin.

165. STEP BACK TO RIDE THE TIGER

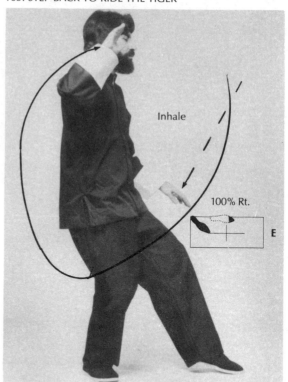

Open the hands; step back to SE with Rt. foot. Shift weight Rt., lower and separate arms, place L. toe in front of Rt. heel; circle and raise Rt. hand near Rt. temple; lower L. hand, brush over L. knee.

165A. A deflects B's kick.

166.

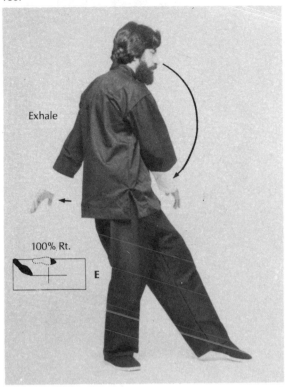

Exhale

100% Rt.

E

Turn waist L. and lower Rt. hand.

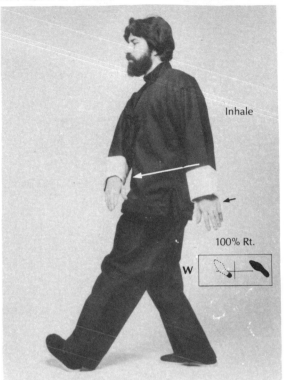

Inhale

100% Rt.

W

Lift L. toe, turn body on ball of Rt. foot 180°. Place L. heel down behind Rt. foot.

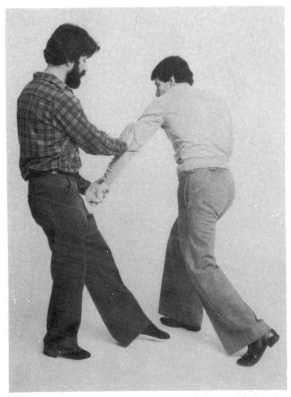

166A. A grabs B's wrist and snaps B's elbow with his Rt. palm.

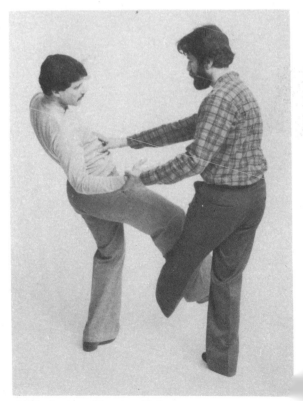

167A. A turns and sweeps B's foot.

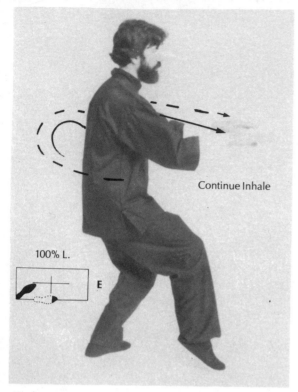

Continue Inhale

100% L.

E

Continue turning, pivoting on L. heel and Rt. toe; shift weight L.; raise Rt. heel; arms follow waist and rise parallel to ground at waist height.

Exhale

100% L.

E

Raise Rt. foot in front of L. shoulder and kick horizontally toward the Rt. (crescent kick in a clockwise circle).

68A. A turns and deflects B's punch.

169A. A kicks B's ribcage.

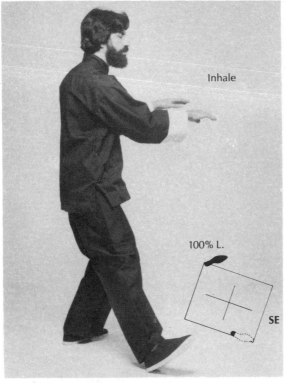

Inhale

100% L.

SE

Drop Rt. shin, keep Rt. thigh parallel to ground. Step out with Rt. heel to form a forward stance (SE).

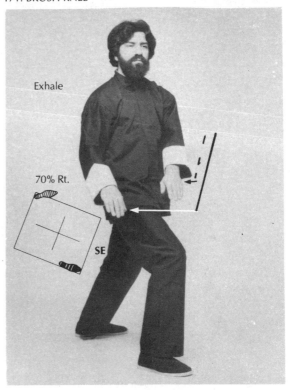

Exhale

70% Rt.

SE

Lower hands; shift weight forward and brush both palms over Rt. knee.

170A. A deflects B's punch.

171A. A pushes B's Rt. arm into B's body.

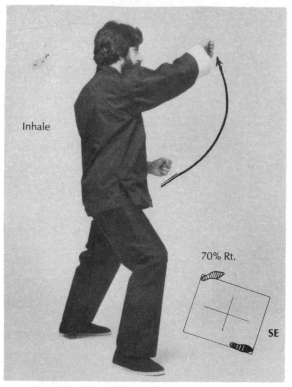

Inhale

70% Rt.

SE

Form two fists; turn waist L.; circle arm counter-clockwise, Rt. arm attacking head level (knuckles inward). L. arm attacking rib level (knuckles outward).

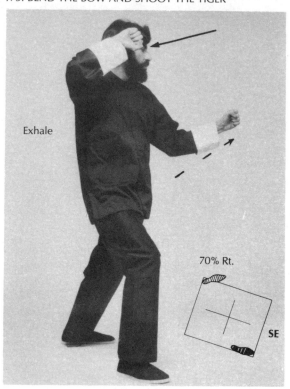

Exhale

70% Rt.

SE

Turn waist Rt.; pull Rt. fist near the Rt. temple; extend L. fist, solar plexus height.

172A. A's L. palm deflects a punch, his Rt. knuckle attacks B's temple.

173A. A punches to B's solar plexus.

Continue Exhale

100% Rt.

SE

Raise L. foot and balance on Rt. foot.

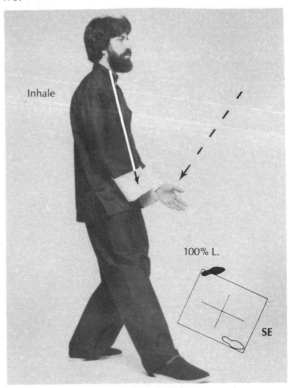

Inhale

100% L.

SE

Place L. foot back to the same spot. Shift weight L.; raise Rt. foot, balance on L. foot; open L. hand. Return Rt. foot to the same spot.

174A. A pulls B's Rt. wrist and punches to his ribs.

175A. A grabs B's wrist and punches his elbow.

176.

Exhale

70% Rt.

E

Shift weight forward.

177. PARRY

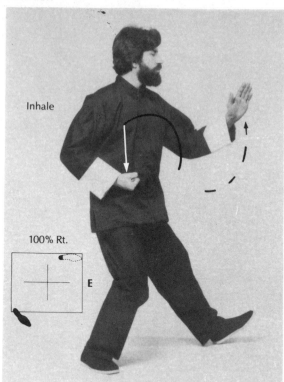

Inhale

100% Rt.

E

Bring L. heel forward, stepping into forward stance. Rt. forearm and fist cross the chest to the Rt. shoulder, then are pulled down near the waist. The L. palm follows the fist to the center of the body.

176A. A grabs B's wrist and snaps his elbow with his L. palm.

177A. A's forearm deflects B's punch; A's L. palm attacks B's head.

178. PUNCH

Exhale

70% L.

E

Shift weight L., the Rt. fist punches center.

179.

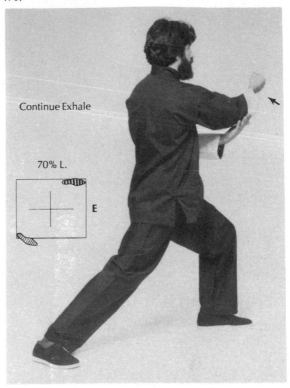

Continue Exhale

70% L.

E

Turn waist 45°L.; place L. palm under Rt. elbow.

178A. A shifts his weight forward and punches; his left arm guards or deflects.

179A. B grabs A's right arm. A's left hand comes underneath B's grasping wrist.

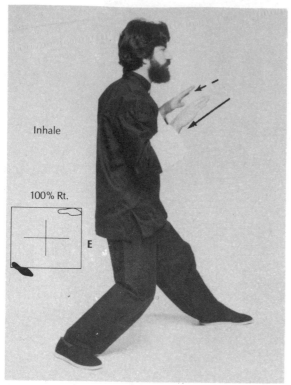

Inhale

100% Rt.

E

Open the Rt. hand, shift weight back and withdraw Rt. arm over L. hand, then both hands turn palms out.

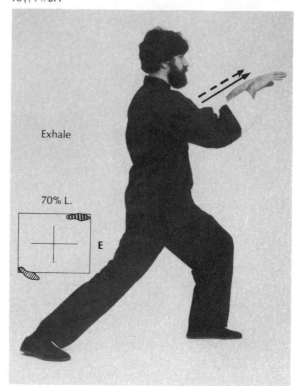

Exhale

70% L.

E

Shift weight forward and push. Arms are parallel.

180A. A's left arm maintains contact with B's arm. Simultaneously, A withdraws his right arm and frees it.

181A. A shifts forward and attacks B's throat or eyes.

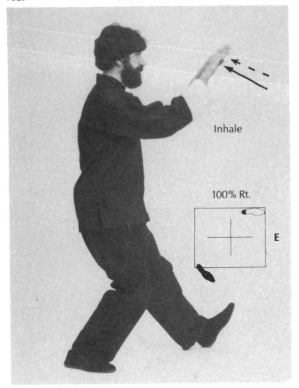

Inhale

100% Rt.

E

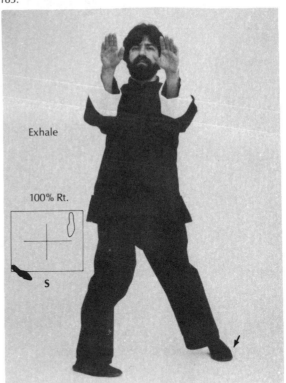

Exhale

100% Rt.

S

Shift weight back; lift L. toe. Pull arms back 45° to the chest.

Turn waist 90° Rt., the L. toe follows pivoting on L. heel. Arms remain parallel.

182A. A's arm deflect's B's punches to the head or chest.

183A. A turns and pulls B's Rt. arm with his Rt. hand. A's L. hand strikes B's head.

184.

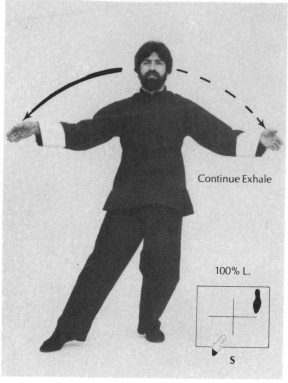

Continue Exhale

100% L.

Shift weight L.; raise Rt. heel; separate hands forming a large arc.

185.

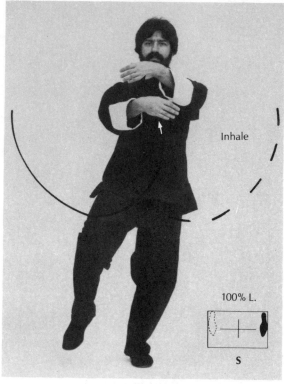

Inhale

100% L.

Arms continue circling downward until they cross each other, L. wrist over R, (continue exhale). Arms move upward to chest height as Rt. foot is raised off the ground (inhale).

185A. A lifts both of B's arms, crossing and tangling them.

187.

Exhale

Continue Exhale

50%-50%

50%-50%

S

S

Rt. foot is placed parallel and shoulders' distance from the L. foot; the L. wrist rests on the Rt. wrist. Arms form a large circle away from the chest.

Lower both hands palms always facing back; middle fingers of both hands are the last points of separation.

186A. A's "Cross Hands" deflect an upward punch.

The Push Hands Form

1. A and B stand facing each other. A's right foot is even with B's right foor and directly in front of B's left foot. A assumes the Ward-off Right posture, with his right arm in front of his chest. B places one palm on A's elbow and one palm on A's wrist.

2. B shifts forward and his left hand pushes A's elbow. A yields by shifting back and turning right. A's left elbow lightly touches B's right elbow.

5. B now assumes the Ward-off Left posture as A places his palm on B's elbow and wrist.

6. A shifts forward and pushes B's elbow. B yields by shifting back and turning to his left. B's right elbow lightly touches A's left elbow.

3. B turns his right palm (towards B's chest) and places his left palm over his right palm.

4. B presses onto A's wrist and A turns left and yields as A's left palm covers B's wrist.

7. A turns his left palm (toward's A's chest) and places his right palm over his left palm.

8. A presses onto B's wrist and B turns right and yields as B's right palm covers A's wrist.

The cycle begins anew as A assumes the Ward-off Right posture again. The exercise should also be done with different variations, i.e. A assumes Ward-off Left posture. Next it should be done with the feet reversed, i.e. A assumes a Left Forward Stance with both the Ward-off Right arm posture and the Ward-off Left posture. In this way one learns to protect and attack in different stances and with different hands.

The object of this exercise is to evade all pushes and presses without stepping back or resisting and to uproot your opponent causing his feet to leave the ground (photographs #9 and 10). (See Push Hands section in "Self Defense" chapter.)

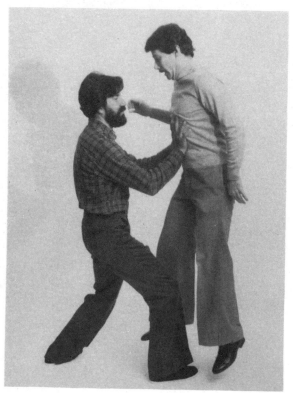

9 Uprooting with the Push

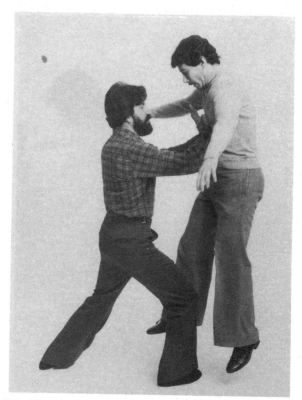

10 Uprooting with the Press

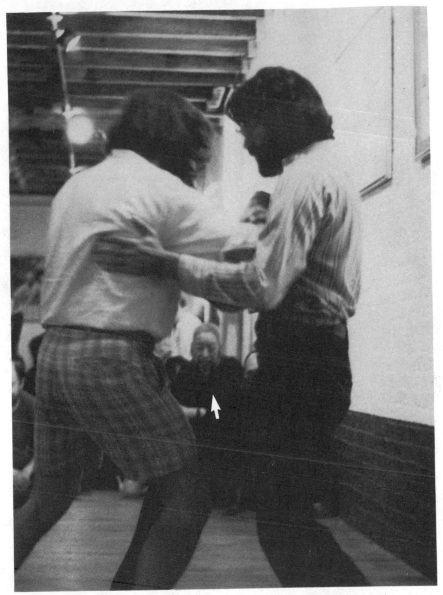

11   The author practicing the Push Hands exercise with the late Grand Master Cheng Man-ch'ing observing, commenting and correcting.

Ta Lu

The most basic Ta Lu set utilizes four postures:

1. Pull

2. Split

These moves are applied in the following manner:

1A. A step forward, grabs B's wrist and pulls him down and slightly to the right.

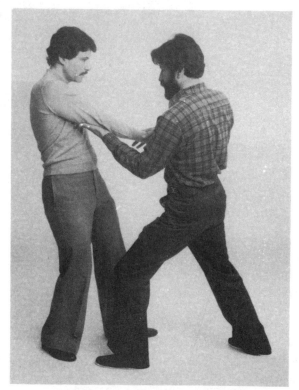

2A. A's Rt. hand pulls B's wrist, while A steps forward and splits B's arm by pushing up at the elbow and pressing down at the wrists.

3. Elbow

4. Shoulder

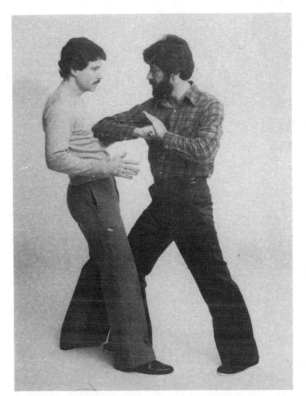

3A. A steps forward and strikes with his elbow to the solar plexus.

4A. A steps forward and strikes B with his shoulder.

When these four moves are combined with Ward-off, Rollback, Press, and Push they correspond to the Pa Qua or eight Trigrams of the *I Ching*. When these eight are added to the postures of the five elements: Advance, Retreat, Look to the Left, Gaze to the Right, and Central Equilibrium, we have the Thirteen Postures.

In Conclusion

Tai Chi Chuan is more than an exercise; it is the physiological expression of Tao. The principles of the Tai Chi Form express Tao and must be understood and practiced daily. When we do this we will improve the quality of our life, creating more harmony for ourselves and for those around us. We are practicing this form and adhering to these principles in order to attain a state which transcends all forms and principles. This is the Tao—The Unchanging Truth. Lao Tzu tells us:

> The great virtue as manifested
> is but following Tao.[1]

Tao is the origin of life and the ultimate goal of life. It is also the ultimate experience of life. The Tai Chi and its principles came forth from the Tao. If we relax, trust and follow these principles, they will lead us back to Tao.

> When the superior scholar is told of Tao,
> He works hard to practice it.
> When the middling scholar is told of Tao,
> It seems that sometimes he keeps it and
> sometimes he loses it.
> When the inferior scholar is told of Tao,
> He laughs aloud at it.[2]

> Let me have sound knowledge and walk on
> the great way (Tao).[3]

You get what you want and you become that which you aspire to become! Therefore, aim for the stars and you will, with patience, perserverance and self-confidence, reach those very heights. As the ancient Sanscrit saying goes, "He who adheres to Brahma becomes Brahma." And as Jesus taught, "Where I am ye also may be."[4] We should have confidence in the great beings that have preceded us and gain inspiration and strength from their words. Then we too can say, as the Buddha did:

> The subject of my meditation is Truth.
> The topic of my conversation is Truth.
> The practice to which I devote myself is Truth.
> For lo! I have become Truth.

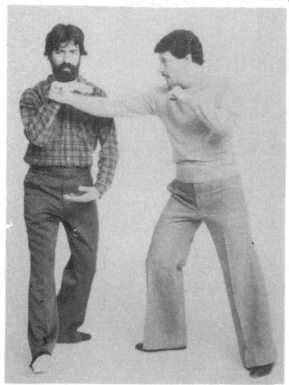

8B. A's turn deflects B's punch.

22B. A turns and blocks B's kick, his Rt. arm is prepared to either block B's punches or attack B's face.

28B. A breaks B's elbow and kicks B's shin.

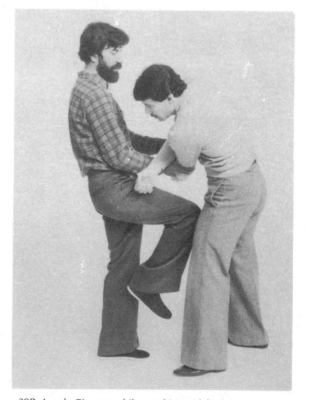

29B. A grabs B's arms while attacking with his knee.

31B. A pulls B's Rt. arm downward.

36B. A deflects B's L. punch and attacks his throat.

43B. A grabs B's wrists and snaps his elbow with his left palm.

52-55 #1

52-55 #2

52-55 #3

52-55 #4

52-55. B grabs A. from behind. A places his right leg behind B's L. leg, shifts to his Rt. leg and trips B.

75B. A's Rt. arm deflects B's punch while A's Rt. fingers are countering to the eyes.

95B. A deflects a punch and kick while countering with a kick.

95C A deflects a punch upward and attacks with his knee to the groin.

97B. A deflects a punch and kick while countering with a kick.

111B. A deflects a punch and strikes to the face.

113B. A deflects a punch and kick.

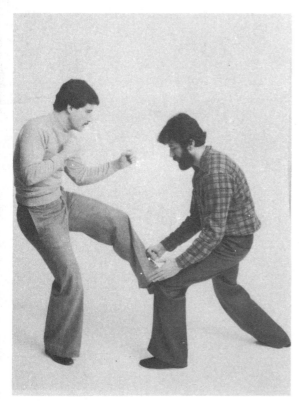

115B. A blocks B's kick with a downward punch.

115C. A deflects a punch and blocks B's kick with a downward punch.

122B. A's L. palm covers B's arm while his Rt. hand deflects B's punch.

132C. A turns, pulling B's Rt. arm and body.

153B. A presses into B's L. side.

165B. A deflects B's kick while kicking B's supporting leg.

165C. A catches B's punches and prepares to trip B.

165D. A pulls B to the L. and pushes his L. leg to the Rt., causing B to trip.

170B. A's lowering arms intercept B's kick.

173B. A catches B's high punch and counter-punches to the ribs.

175B. A grabs B's wrist and punches his stomach.

177B. A deflects B's punch with his L. palm and prepares to counter-punch.

Footnotes

Chapter 1. Tai Chi—The Supreme Ultimate
1. Yin—the dark half of the Tai Chi symbol. It represents the receptive, yielding, feminine principle.
2. Yang—the light half of the Tai Chi symbol. It represents the creative, firm, masculine principle.

Chapter 2. Origin and History
1. Due to limited space I cannot list all the Tai Chi experts who also deserve mention. I have listed just a few, who are also authors of Tai Chi books.
2. *I Ching*, Wilhelm translation, Bollington Series, Princeton University Press, Princeton, New Jersey, 1967, p. 185.
3. Trigrams—a symbol with three lines which represents one of eight directions and/or conditions of change in the cosmos.

Chapter 3. The Tai Chi Classics
1. See *Bibliography of Tai Chi Chuan Books*.
2. Tan Tien—a point about two inches below the navel. It is the center of movement and the storehouse of Chi.
3. In addition to "Before the Gate of Heaven Breathing" there exists "After the Gate of Heaven Breathing" which consists of contracting the stomach when one inhales and expanding it when one exhales.

Chapter 4. Philosophy
1. *Tao Te Ching*, Ch'u Ta-Kao translation, Samuel Weiser Inc., New York, Chapter 1, p. 11.
2. *I Ching*, Wilhelm translation, *Ta Chuan*, p. 301.
3. Paul Tillich, Bishop and theologian, defines God as the Ground of being or Ultimate Reality. With such a definition, it becomes unnecessary to debate the existence of God—debate could concern itself only with the nature of this Ultimate Relity.
4. Tao Te Ching, K.O. Smith translation, Chapter 51, p. 11.
5. *Tao Te Ching*, Ch'u Ta-Kao translation, Chapter 1, p. 11.
6. *I Ching*, Wilhelm translation.
7. Ibid, p. 297.
8. Ibid, Introduction, p. 1
9. Ibid, p. liii.
10. Ibid, p. xxxiii.
11. Ibid, p. xxiv.
12. Ibid, p. xxxiv
13. Ibid, p. xxxiv.
14. Ibid, p. 137.
15. Ibid, p. 140.
16. *Tao Te Ching*, K.O. Smith translation, p. 9.
17. Ibid.
18. *Tao Te Ching*, Ch'u Ta-Kao translation, Chapter XXIX, p. 42.
19. Ibid, Chapter LXIII, p. 78.
20. *The Tai Chi Classics* are explained in an earlier chapter. See also *Bibliography*.
21. *Tao Te Ching*, Ch'u Ta-Kao translation, Chapter LXXVIII, p. 93.
22. Ibid, Chapter LXXVI, p. 91.

Chapter 5. Spirituality
1. *Tao Te Ching*, Ch'u Ta-Kao translation, Chapter XXII, p. 34.
2. Ibid, Chapter XXVIII, p. 40.
3. Ibid, Chapter XLIX, p. 64.
4. Ibid, Chapter XLVI, p. 61.
5. Ibid, Ch. XLIX, p. 64.
6. *New Testament*, Matthew 16:24; Mark 8:34; Luke 9:23.
7. *The Way of the Pilgrim*, H. Bacovcin translation, Image Books, Garden City, N.J., 1978. p. 7.
8. The right side of the body is yang—positive; the left side is yin—negative. See also acupuncture and polarity massage.
9. See *Zen and the Art of Archery*, E. Henigel, Random House, New York, 1973.
10. So Hum—a mantra meaning "I am That."

Chapter 6. Tai Chi Chuan and Other Eastern Systems
1. *I Ching,* The Great Treatise, Wilhelm translation, p. 281.
2. Ibid, p. 280.
3. Ibid, p. 282.
4. Hara—the vital center, located in the stomach cavity. The Japanese term *Hara* corresponds to the Tan Tien, however, the *hara* is a slightly larger area.

Chapter 7. Tai Chi Chuan and Western Philosophy
1. *Analytical Psychology: Its Theory and Practice,* Lecture No. 1, Carl Jung; Pantheon Books, New York, 1968.
2. *The Psychology of Consciousness,* R.E. Ornstein; W.H. Freeman and Co., San Francisco, 1972.
3. *The Systematic Desensitization Treatment of Phobias,* Joseph Wolpe, American Journal of Psychiatry, 1963.
4. *The Function of the Orgasm,* Wilhelm Reich, Farrar Straus and Giroux, New York, 1973.

Chapter 8. Tai Chi Chuan and Occult Systems
1. Hermes Trismegistus. See *The Secret Teachings of All Ages,* Manly P. Hall; The Philosophical Research Society, Los Angeles, 1945, p. xxxvii.
2. The Symbolism of the Tarot, P.D. Ouspensky; Dover Publications, New York, 1976, p. 7.

Chapter 9. Tai Chi Chuan and Health
1. Kirlian photography—a type of photography invented by Mr. Kirlian which can photograph the energy surrounding bodies.
2. *Behavioral Kinesiology,* John Diamond; Harper & Row, New York, 1979, p. 28.
3. Ibid, p. 25.
4. This statement concerns the "long form" which takes about twenty-five minutes to do.
5. *Nuclear Madness,* Dr. Helen Caldicott; Autumn Press, 1978.
6. This is corroborated in the 1977 report made by the "Select Committee on Nutrition" headed by Senator George McGovern.
7. *The Tao of Sex,* Ishirhara & Levy; Harper & Row, New York, 1968. See also *Sexual Secrets,* Douglas & Slinger; Destiny Books, New York, 1979.
8. *Analytical Psychology: Its Theory and Practice,* Lecture No. 3, Carl Jung; Pantheon Books, New York, 1968. See also *Two Essays on Analytical Psychology,* Carl Jung (Collected Works, Volume 7, Par. 296 ff.); Bollingen Series, Princeton University Press, Princeton, N.J. See also *The Way of All Women,* Esther Harding.
9. *The Chinese Art of Healing,* Palos; Bantam Books, New York, 1972, p. 144.
10. Ibid, p. 145.
11. Ibid, p. 146.
12. Ibid, p. 148.
13. Ibid, p. 149-150.
14. *Rehabilitation World Journal,* p. 23.
15. For further information on the workings of the E.K.G. and how it is used as a diagnostic tool see *Rapid Interpretations of E.K.G.,* Dubin, 2nd Edition, Cover Pub. Co., Tampa, Florida, 1970.
16. *Exercise Testing and Training of Individuals with Heart Disease: A Handbook for Physicians* by Committee on Exercises, published by A.H.A., Dallas, Texas, 1975, p. 25. See also *Exercise Your Way to Fitness and Heart Health,* Lenore Zohman, M.D.; Mazola Oil Co., Coventry, Connecticut, 1974, p. 11.

Chapter 10. Tai Chi and Self-Defense
1. Some of these remarkable stories are retold in *Tai Chi: The "Supreme Ultimate" Exercise for Health, Sport, and Self-Defense* by Cheng Man-ching and Robert W. Smith, and in *Tai Chi Chuan for Health and Self-Defense* by T.T. Liang.
2. It was my great fortune to study the Two Person Form with Master T.T. Liang and I understand that he is preparing a series of films and instruction on this wonderful exercise for interested students.

Chapter 11. Conclusion
1. *Tao Te Ching,* Ch'u Ta-Kao translation, p. 33.
2. Ibid, p. 56.
3. Ibid, p. 68.
4. *The New Testament,* John 14:3.

Bibliography of Tai Chi Chuan Books

Chen, William C.C., *Tai Chi Chuan,* W.C.C. Chen School of Tai Chi Chuan, New York, 1973.

Chen, Yearning K., *Tai Chi, Its Effects and Practical Applications,* Unicorn Press, Hong Kong, 1971.

*Cheng Man-ch'ing, *Tai Chi Chuan,* Shih Chung Tai Chi Center, Taipei, 1963.

*Cheng Man-ch'ing & R. Smith, *Tai-Chi,* C.E. Tuttle Co., Rutland, Vermont, 1971.

Da Liu, *Tai Chi Ch'uan and I Ching,* Harper & Row, New York, 1972.

Huang, Wen-Shan, *Fundamentals of Tai Chi Ch'uan,* South Sky Book Co., Hong Kong, 1973.

Kauz, Herman, *Tai Chi Handbook,* Dolphin Books, Doubleday & Co., Garden City, N.Y. 1974.

Kuo, Lien-ying, *Tai Chi Chuan, Theory and Practice,* Taipei, Taiwan. Available from the author, 11 Brenham Place, San Francisco, California.

*Lee, Ying-arng, *Tai Chi for Health,* Unicorn Press, Hong Kong, 1968.

*Liang, T.T., *Tai Chi Chuan for Health and Self-Defence,* Vintage Books, New York, 1974.

*Lo Inn Amacker Foe, (trans.) *The Essence of Tai Chi Chuan,* North Atlantic Books, Richmond, California, 1979.

*These books contain translations of the *Tai Chi Classics.*

General Bibliography

Bahm, Archie J., *Yoga, Union with the Ultimate,* Frederick Ungar Publishing Co., New York, 1964.

Beau, Georges, *Chinese Medicine,* Avon Books, New York, 1972.

Blackney, R.B. (trans.) *Tao Teh Ching* (Lao Tzu), Mentor Books, New York, 1955.

Bacovcin, H., *The Way of the Pilgrim,* Image Books, Garden City, New York, 1978.

Buddha, *Sayings of Buddha,* Peter Pauper Press, Mt. Vernon, New York, 1957.

Burtt, E.A., *The Teachings of the Compassionate Buddha,* Mentor Books, New York, 1955.

Caldicott, Dr. Helen, *Nuclear Madness,* Autumn Press, Brookline, Massachusetts, 1978.

Chang, Jolan, *The Tao of Love and Sex,* E.P. Dutton, New York, 1977.

Chow, David and Richard Spangler, *King Fu, History, Philosophy and Technique,* Doubleday & Co., Garden City, New York, 1977.

Committee on Exercises, *Exercise Testing and Training of Individuals with Heart Disease: A Handbook for Physicians,* A.H.A. Dallas, 1975.

Conze, Edward, *Buddhist Scriptures,* Penguin Books, Baltimore, Maryland, 1968.

Diamond, John, *Behavioral Kinesiology,* Harper & Row, New York, 1979.

Douglas, Nik, *Tantra Yoga,* Munshiram Manoharlal, New Delhi, 1971.

Douglas, Nik, & Penny Slinger, *Sexual Secrets,* Destiny Books, New York, 1979.

Draeger, *Asian Fighting Arts,* Medallion Books, Berkeley, California, 1974.

Eliade, Mircea, *Patanjali and Yoga,* Schocken Books, New York, 1976.

Hall, Manly P., *The Secret Teachings of All Ages,* The Philosophical Research Society, Los Angeles, California, 1945.

Henigel, E., *Zen and the Art of Archery,* Random House, New York, 1973.

Huard, P., & M. Wong, *Chinese Medicine,* World University Library, New York, 1968.

Humana, Charles & Wang Wu, *The Chinese Way of Love,* Avon Books, New York, 1971.

Jung, Carl, *Analytical Psychology: Its Theory and Practice,* Pantheon Books, New York, 1968.

Jung, Carl, *On Synchronicity, Man and Time,* Bollingen Series XXX, Pantheon Books, New York, 1951.

Jung, Carl, *Synchronicity: An Acausal Connecting Principle,* Bollingen, New York, 1955.

Kapleau, Philip, *The Three Pillars of Zen,* Beacon Press, Boston, 1965.

Lawson-Wood, D. & J., *Five Elements of Acupuncture and Chinese Massage,* Health Science Press, England, 1975.

Leong, L. *Acupuncture: a Layman's View,* Signet Books, New York, 1974.

Levi & Ishihara, *The Tao of Sex,* Harper Books, New York, 1974.

Lu K'uan Yu, *Ch'an and Zen Teachings,* Samuel Weiser, Inc., New York, 1962.

Lu K'uan Yu, *the Secrets of Chinese Meditation,* Samuel Weiser, Inc., New York, 1969.

Lu K'uan Yu, *Taoist Yoga, Alchemy and Immortality,* Samuel Weiser, Inc. 1973.

Manaka, Y. & I. Urquhart, *The Layman's Guide to Acupuncture,* Weatherhill, Inc., New York, 1973.

Mann, Felix, *Acupuncture the Ancient Chinese Art of Healing,* Random House, New York, 1963.

Medeiros, Earl C., *The History and Philosophy of Kung Fu,* C.E. Tuttle Co., Inc., Rutland, Vermont, 1974.

Minick, Michael, *The Wisdom of Kung Fu,* Michael Dempsey, London, 1974.

Murphy, J. *Secrets of the I. Ching,* Parker Publishing Co., New York, 1970.

Ohsawa, G. *Acupuncture and the Philosophy of the Far East,* Tao Publishing, Boston, 1973.

Ornstein, R.E., *The Psychology of Consciousness,* W.H. Freeman and Co., San Francisco, 1972.

Ouspensky, R.D., *The Symbolism of the Tarot,* Dover Publications, New York, 1976.

Palos, Stephan, *The Chinese Art of Healing,* Bantam Books, New York, 1972.

Reich, Wilhelm, *The Function of the Orgasm,* Farrar, Straus and Giroux, New York, 1973.

Ribner, Susan and Dr. Richard Chin, *The Martial Arts,* Harper & Row, New York, 1978.

Russel, E., *Spiritual Guidance in Contemporary Taoism,* Spiritual Disciplines, Bollingen Series XXX 4, Pantheon Books, New York, 1951.

Smith, R.W., *Chinese Boxing, Methods and Masters,* C.E. Tuttle Co. Inc., Rutland, Vermont, 1967.

Smith, R.W., *Hsing-i,* Kodansha International, New York, 1974.

Smith, R.W., *Pa-Kua,* Kodansha International, New York, 1977.

Suzuki, D.T. *The Zen Monk's Life,* Olympia Press, Inc., New York, 1972.

Waley, A., *The Way and Its Power,* Grove Press, New York, 1958.

Watson, B., *Chuang Tzu: Basic Writings,* Columbia University Press, New York, 1964.

Wilhelm, R., *The Secret of the Golden Flower,* Harvest Books, New York, 1962.

Wilhelm, R., *The I Ching or Book of Changes,* The Richard Wilhelm translation rendered into English by Cary F. Baynes. Bollingen Series XIX, Copyright 1950, 1967 and 1977 by Princeton University Press, Princeton, N J

Wolpe, Joseph *The Systematic Desensitization Treatment of Phobias,* American Journal of Psychiatry, 1963.

Wu Wei-P'ing, *Chinese Acupuncture,* Health Science Press, Northamtonshire, England, 1973.

Zohman, Lenore, M.D., *Exercise Your Way to Fitness and Heart Health,* Mazola Oil Co., Coventry, Connecticutt, 1974.

Two valuable learning tools for the serious Tai Chi student are:
1. A cassette tape of the author teaching, with a step by step description of the moves pictured in this book,
2. A super 8mm color film of the author performing the Yang style of Tai Chi Form.

For information please write:
Lawrence Galante
School of Tai Chi Chuan and Related Oriental Studies
209 1st Avenue
New York, N.Y. 10003